Never Take Money From A Stranger

"How Knowing Your Customer Leads To Sales Success"

By Chuck Reaves

KENDALL/HUNT PUBLISHING COMPANY
2460 Kerper Boulevard P.O. Box 539 Dubuque, Iowa 52004-0539

Contents

INTRODUCTION 1

Chapter One

The Essence of the Story 9

Two

Taking Control 23

Three

How to Ask a Question 49

Four

Advanced Questioning Techniques 69

Five

Non-Retailing 93

Six

The Only Question You'll
Ever Have to Answer 109

Preface

"You have not because you ask not and even when you ask, you ask amiss: you ask with selfish intent."

James 4:2

The first time I heard a speaker say, "You can have anything you want out of life," I said to myself, "Yeah, Right." Once I heard myself say the exact same words to someone else, I realized I had come full circle.

There are many elements to attaining what you want out of life. This book deals with one of them: asking for what you want. Once you have decided what your current objective is in life, go for it. Find out who the people are who know what you need to know and *ask* them for knowledge. Find out who the people are who can help you and *ask* them to help.

Discovering that *asking the right questions the right way* was also the key to great customer service and resulted in greater sales success, was another illuminating concept. If you are in sales, and who isn't, you need to study the techniques in this book. When you ask the right question the right way of the right person, you will be amazed at the results.

This book will teach you what you need to know to be more confident and more successful in asking for whatever you want. What it will not do is do the asking for you. Take the principles and techniques from this book and apply them in your life and business right now. Wherever you are, whatever you are doing, use what you learn and watch the world miraculously change.

Introduction

There I was on the beach at Acapulco, sipping something cool and frothy out of a tall glass. It was a delicious conclusion to a hot and heavy sales campaign; the trip was a reward for being the top producer out of 1,100 salespeople in my division. I had earned it, and I had come a long way.

At one time I had worked as a technician for AT&T, wore blue jeans and a flannel shirt to work, and carried my lunch in a paper sack. My ten-year marriage had ended, I was broke, living in a house with almost no plumbing and driving an old Buick sedan with dents.

It was hard to believe how fast I was getting nowhere. There were people around me who had more, did more and enjoyed life more, though they were no smarter than I was. People with less seniority got the promotions where I worked, people who arrived later got better tables in the restaurants where I ate. There seemed to be a privileged class out there and I was not part of it.

I was disgusted. I didn't know what I wanted out of life or how to get it, but I knew I didn't want more of the same. I began to read everything I could find, listened to anyone who would talk to me, and in the process I learned the techniques I use to achieve what I have today.

What do I do today? I am a successful business consultant, sales trainer, motivational speaker and author. There's no obvious reason for me to have become so accomplished, because I lack the education and experience of my peers, I'm not a good socializer—I don't drink or play golf—and I knew nothing about sales when I was promoted into the job.

Did I accomplish it overnight? No, it took hard work to sharpen those skills. It's true that the material things in my life improved, but what's more important is that I improved. Instead of being content with whatever fell into my lap, I decided what I wanted and found a way to get it.

Is this a get-rich-quick program? There's no such thing. Only you can decide what success means for you, and only you can determine when you want it. The process described in this book is an option, and it is available to you whenever you want to use it.

I always believed that my lack of education and social skills were a handicap, but those deficiencies turned out to be insignificant compared to what I do have—a love of people. You might even say that all I know is people, and that what I learned in my quest to change my life is how to use people skills. It is a concept so simple to describe and so difficult to execute that little has been written about it.

When I realized how many people could benefit from this process, I thought about writing a textbook. Then a friend said, "Do you like to read textbooks, Chuck?"

"No," I admitted.

"Would anyone else? Why would you write a textbook?"

"Well, how could I write about it?" I asked.

"You're such a good yarn spinner," said my friend, "why don't you write a story book."

I thought a long time about that conversation, and I decided that my friend was right. I knew then that I would write "my kind of book" so I could pass on these skills, in my own way, to those who wish to know.

This is my kind of book. You will find it full of information about the processes and techniques you will need to accomplish whatever you want. You will also find a yarn, an ongoing story running like a thread through each of the chapters and, to get us started, I'll begin it here.

The Story Begins ...

With the top down and the speedometer hovering around 80 MPH, Bruce's BMW325i was providing the perfect atmosphere for him and Amy. The hot summer sun was improving their tanning-bed tans, and made their Varnet sunglasses all the more appropriate.

Conversation was impossible with the wind in their faces, so Bruce's mind had wandered in one direction and Amy's in another. Bruce was thinking about the family reunion, the purpose for this trip. He was wondering how all the folks back home would react to his obvious success. He wondered if they would be a little envious, or maybe very envious. He wondered how Amy would react when she saw the humble beginnings from which he had pulled himself. She would have to be impressed, he thought.

Amy was wondering what it would take to get a commitment out of Bruce. They had been dating for almost two years and his original excuses were no longer valid. First he wanted to get established with a major clothing designer, then he wanted to wait for a promotion or two. Next he wanted to buy a co-op. She was sure that Bruce was serious about her, but she just couldn't get him down that aisle.

Once Bruce pulled off the interstate highway onto the county road, Amy asked if they could stop for something to drink. They stopped at a country store that had modern refrigerator and freezer cases in a simple building. Most of the people turned and watched as the two of them walked in. Amy liked that. Many of the men continued to stare at the car, and Bruce liked that.

"What would you like, Amy?" Bruce was putting his sunglasses on top of his head.

"Do you think they have Perrier?"

Bruce had not been back here for several years, and did not know how sophisticated the people might have become. "I don't know. I'll ask."

Bruce walked into the store and asked the man behind the counter, "Perrier?"

The man stared at Bruce without changing the expression on his face. "No," he said, "Harvey J. Johnson. Don't know any Perry A. Fact of the matter is, I don't know any Perry at all in these parts."

Bruce was not sure what to say, but that was not a problem, because the man continued. "Now there'us a feller here about six year ago who went by the name of Berry, but I believe that would have been his last name."

The man stopped talking because Bruce had returned to the front of the store. "What would be your second choice?" he said to Amy.

"I'll go look myself," Amy said as she pulled open the screen door.

In a few minutes they were standing in the Georgia sun with chilled bottles of soda. While Bruce put gas in the car, Amy asked him again what she should expect at the reunion.

"Well, don't expect a whole lot. Most of these people have not traveled much, they live in their own world and, for the most part, they're very happy."

"Will they like me?" Amy was checking her makeup in the side mirror on the car.

"Actually, they like pretty much everybody. It's a much simpler lifestyle than the one we live in the city. It's really kind of nice."

"But awfully, uh, rural, don't you think?" She did not want Bruce harboring any ideas about extending their visit.

"Oh, yeah, it's rural all right." He finished pumping the gas and was returning the hose to the pump. "We'll just visit for awhile, let you meet my family and we'll head back to Atlanta. What time is your flight?"

"Eleven something. I won't be back at the apartment until nearly two in the morning. The things I do for you.

Claude had made up his mind. He was leaving for the big city.

Until recently, all Claude ever wanted to do was hunt and fish. His cousin Bruce had returned to Clarkesville for the Thompson family reunion over the Fourth of July weekend, and that's when Claude's perspective had changed. Bruce was driving a BMW convertible, he had great clothes, a gold watch, and a lovely blond on his arm.

The image Bruce cultivated was one Claude had seen before, but always on television, never in real life. It occurred to him that if Bruce could do it, so could he. After all, he and Bruce had grown up in the same small town, they had spent many afternoons in the woods chasing rabbit and deer and, in many other respects, they were very much alike.

Of course Bruce had excelled in school and had earned a scholarship to the university. After college he had several offers from major corporations, each one a little better than the last. He had settled in New York working for Genre, the hottest fashion house in the country.

Still, Bruce fit right in with the "home folks" at the picnic, and before leaving Clarkesville Bruce spent a few minutes talking with his cousin.

"Claude, I'd like you to meet my friend, Amy." Amy had already met more people than she wanted to, and she had purposely not remembered any of their names. It was apparent to everyone that she would rather be somewhere else.

Claude stuck his hand out toward Amy, and she heard him say, "Hire you?"

"No thanks, I have a job," she answered.

Bruce spoke up, "No, Honey, 'How are you,' 'hire you,' get it?"

Amy was looking at Bruce as he spoke. She turned back to face Claude with a brief, disinterested smile. "Oh. Sorry. Fine, how are you?"

"So, Claude, what are you going to do with yourself?" Bruce asked.

"Ya mean right now?" Claude asked.

"No, I mean what kind of career, uh, job are you thinking about looking for?" Bruce had to remember to ask questions in a way that would be easy for Claude to understand.

Claude thought for a moment and answered, "Well, I was gonna work in the mill or at th' lumber yard, but both of them's shuttin' down, ya' know." He looked over at Bruce's car. " 'Sides, I think I'd rather work in the city like you and drive one of them fancy sports cars like 'at. What do you do anyway?"

It wasn't going to be easy to explain to Claude what a Director of Marketing does. "My title is Director of Marketing. I help my company decide what will sell and how to sell it."

Claude thought that sounded like a boring, do-nothing job. If somebody in New York would pay that kind of money for what Bruce was doing, imagine what they would pay a hard worker like himself, Claude thought.

"Are there any openings at your company, Bruce?"

"It's a big company, Claude, there are always openings for the right people." Bruce shifted his eyes to Amy and winked.

"Maybe I should come up there to New York and look for work." Claude was looking for some kind of an invitation from Bruce.

"Yeah, right." Bruce was standing up and reached out to help his date stand. "Amy and I need to head out. I have a meeting in Atlanta tomorrow and she's catching a flight to LaGuardia tonight."

"LaGuardia? Where's that?" Claude asked.

"New York, Claude. It's an airport in New York."

Amy couldn't keep quiet any longer. "Where have you been all of your life?"

Claude answered, "Rat cheer."

Amy looked at Bruce as he mouthed the words, "Right here."

"You've never been away from this area?"

"Ass rat."

Again Amy looked at Bruce. "That's right," he echoed.

"Well," Claude continued, "there was one trip I made to Atlanta, but I don't talk much about that."

"Neither, I bet, do the people in Atlanta," Amy thought to herself. "So, you've never been to New York?"

"No'm," Claude responded.

Amy thought for a minute, looked at Bruce and asked, "That's 'no ma'am,' right?"

Bruce smiled and nodded.

"We need to be going, Bruce." Amy was on her feet.

Claude stood up and said, "Well, have a safe trip. I'll look you up if I ever get up your way. It'us great seein' y'all, Bruce."

Claude walked with them to their car, partly to be polite and partly to get a better look at the BMW. Bruce was pleased when he saw how Claude eyed the car. Bruce asked if Claude would like to drive the car, but Claude declined, afraid he might scratch it. Bruce did talk him into going for a short ride in it. Amy sat in the back seat rather than have to stay behind and make conversation with the locals.

Back at the picnic, Claude got out, thanked Bruce for the ride and said goodbye to his cousin and to Amy. As they drove out of Clarkesville, Amy turned to Bruce and said, "It's hard to imagine that you grew up in that environment."

"Oh, Claude's all right. He'll never amount to much, but he'll be happy. Clarkesville is all he's ever known."

"You mean he's never been out of Clarkesville?" Amy asked.

"Not exactly. He went to Atlanta once for a weekend with some of his friends. It was a disaster. Maybe I'll tell you the story sometime. At any rate, he's never lived anywhere but here."

"Maybe you should invite him up to visit, Bruce. You know, show him the city. . . ." Amy was testing to see if Bruce was interested in entertaining his cousin. After all, Bruce did like to show off. Her comment was interrupted by Bruce's laugh.

"You don't know Claude. He wouldn't last a day in New York." Bruce continued to laugh as he thought about Claude in New York.

The Essence of the Story

Maybe it's because I'm a slow learner. Perhaps it's because I'm so stubborn. I was in my thirties, in the same entry-level job I had hired into ten years earlier, going nowhere.

When I began to question *why,* I started a process that changed my life, a process that can change yours, and one that you can teach to others. I can set out the essence of the process in one sentence, but you'll need the principles and techniques explained later in this book to make it work for you.

The best explanation of the process is this:

We Don't Have What We Want Because We Don't Ask For It, and Even When We Ask, We Don't Ask Properly

A story will illustrate what I mean. A man died and went to heaven. He was met at the Gate by Saint Peter, who took him on a tour of heaven. At one point they walked up to a building that was larger than a football field and four stories high. Saint Peter put his weight behind a huge door and pushed it open. They entered and Saint Peter closed the door behind them. As they walked the length of the building, the man saw that it was a warehouse stacked to the ceiling with boxes.

The man turned to Saint Peter and asked, "What's in all these boxes?"

Saint Peter answered, "These are the blessings we had for you that you never asked for."

The truth is that there are many things available for us that we never receive because we never ask. For instance, right now I am sitting in an airplane using a laptop computer that I have because I asked for it. I bought a coach ticket and I'm sitting in first class because I asked for it. The flight attendant just brought me a deck of cards because I asked for it. No one else has asked, and no one else has a fresh deck of cards.

What was it like for you on your last flight? Did you get a deck of cards? They were there for the asking.

You may say that a deck of cards is a small thing, and it is, but it illustrates an important point. If we don't ask for the simplest things, are we even aware of the greater things that might be there for the asking? In other words, if you weren't willing to request the cards it's probably a safe bet that you didn't ask for the upgrade to first class, and that you never even thought of asking for a computer.

> Would you like to be a better manager?
> A better parent or spouse?
> A better salesperson or sales manager?
> Would you like to be more successful?

If you're like most people, your answer to these questions is *yes.*

Will you start asking for the things you want?

If you're like most people, your answer to this question is *no.*

Why We Don't Ask

Why are people reluctant to ask for what they want? There are several reasons, and the first one is *rejection.* We all dread being rejected. It's the reason salespeople will not ask for the order. It's the reason a guy will not ask a girl to go out, even though they are strongly attracted to each other. Funny, isn't it?

If you know of an item you would like to buy, but you can only buy it from a salesperson who asks for the order, you will probably still have your money a year from now and you will not have the item. People would rather fail than be rejected.

We gave that assignment to the students in a sales training program. They were to shop for a specific item and buy it from the salesperson who asked for the order. The members of one team decided that they would buy a shirt for the instructor—I really liked that! At one store the salesperson helped them find the perfect shirt, and the team members took turns saying that the recipient would be sure to like it. The salesperson listened and said nothing. Finally, in desperation, one of the students said, "Look, we're in a sales training course and we have to buy something from a salesperson who asks for the order. We'd like to buy this shirt from you but we can't unless you ask us to buy it." They came back empty-handed.

Another reason we fail to ask for what we want is that it requires *patience*. Even after reading and understanding the ideas in this book you'll probably still want to "tell" rather than ask. It's instinctive and it seems to work faster. It doesn't, but it seems faster at first to shout out an order than to sell a person on an idea. However, once you've used this process for a few weeks, it will seem natural and effortless. You may even find yourself having to develop patience for people who don't ask.

Finally, we don't ask because it requires us to use the least exercised, most out-of-shape part of our body: *our brain*. It's much easier to react than to act, to force things into an existing mold than to make a mold to fit the need.

Questions Make Us Think

We're creatures of habit. All our lives have been spent programming our minds to respond to certain stimuli in certain ways. Sometimes that's good, because it saves time and effort. Sometimes it's not.

For example, we have trained ourselves to pull our hands back when we touch something hot. That's good. We've also trained ourselves to give superficial, rote answers to inquiries and to accept those answers from others. These are habits that can and should be broken.

The kindest thing we can do for friends and strangers alike is to make them think. Read that sentence again, it's important. When people are forced to think, they learn. Even when they're thinking about something that happened in the past or something that recurs over and over again, thinking about it can bring new insights.

In the chapters that follow you will see how asking seemingly obvious questions caused my clients to rethink their businesses and achieve greater success than they had imagined they could. You will also see how individuals, when asked in the right way to explain what they were doing and why, found themselves changing their lives and pursuing their dreams with renewed enthusiasm and energy.

One of the greatest compliments I can receive is, "Well, you got me thinking." As a consultant I am most effective when I enable others to develop their own solutions. It is true that I can visualize my clients' problems, and in my mind I can develop some solutions. If I tell them my ideas they learn a little. If I coach them through the process, they will arrive at solutions that are different from mine, they will learn much more, and so will I. It's much more gratifying to teach clients how to think than to continue taking their money to do their thinking for them.

You've heard the old adage, "Give a man a fish and he will eat for a day; teach him to fish and he will eat forever." Asking questions will cause people to think; asking questions effectively will cause them to think more deeply and imaginatively than ever.

Throughout this book you will find tips for effective questioning. Because they're important, we have set them apart from the rest of the text so you can find them easily while using this book as a resource. Here's the first one:

TIP #1

The Human Mind Cannot Not Respond To A Question

Whenever we are asked a question we respond, mentally and physically, because we have been trained all our lives to do so. We are also conditioned to respond differently to different types of questions.

For instance, most people listen closely to a question, wanting to make sure they understand it. They lean forward and look at you intently. This is a conditioned response.

On the other hand, in stressful business and legal situations, some people will respond to a question by acting as if they never heard it. They rock back and forth in their chair, staring at the interrogator as the question is asked, continuing to rock and stare but never answering. This is also a result of conditioning, responding by not responding.

What does a Hershey bar look like? See? Right now you have a Hershey bar on your mind, because you reacted automatically out of lifelong conditioning. You may still be holding this book the same way, and your body may not have moved at all, but you're thinking about a Hershey bar. The human mind cannot not respond to a question. Using the question put the image I wanted in your mind. I can even plant the color "silver" in your mind by asking about the colors of the letters on the Hershey bar wrapper. You cannot stop your mind from going to work when it hears a question. Neither can your customers, your coworkers or the members of your family.

Ignorance Leads to Knowledge

When I was selling for AT&T, I frequently found myself in situations where I lacked the knowledge and experience I needed. In those circumstances I started asking questions, and soon I had all the information I could use. As one question led to another, my clients would begin the thinking process which led them to new ideas and conclusions. The excitement this generated caused them to associate me with their new ideas. All I did was ask some questions. The new ideas came from them, but I took the credit anyway!

I had not consciously adopted a questioning role because I thought it was the smart thing to do. I had stumbled onto the process out of ignorance, because I didn't know what else to do. If I had possessed a little knowledge, or if my knowledge had equaled that of my client, nothing new would have happened. We would have had the same old conversation the client always had with other people.

Think about that for a minute. When you and your associates meet, doesn't the conversation tend to follow a predictable pattern? What if you brought in a person who had little or no knowledge about the subject you were discussing. Would the conversation change as you tried to include the new individual?

TIP #2

A.A.I.
Always Assume Ignorance

Always assume that you and the other person are ignorant, and that more information is available than either of you possess. This will not only encourage you to ask questions, it will help you to formulate the questions you need to ask.

When we think we know the answers, we describe them. If we need to know something, we ask questions. If we assume that the customer hasn't considered everything, our inquiry leads us in new directions.

When good salespeople stop producing it is usually because they have fallen into a behavior trap and they're making "rookie errors." They're not planning properly, they've stopped asking for the order, or they're "winging it" in other ways. One of the most effective ways to bring them out of the slump is to ask them to work with a rookie. The interaction between a veteran and a rookie is a great way to revitalize old ideas and to generate new ones. Have your seasoned salesperson ask the rookie this question: "How do you think you did?" The conversation that follows will enlighten both of them.

Maybe you're thinking, "That's great for salespeople, but not for me. I'm not in sales." Think again. Everybody is in sales. In fact, there are only two types of people in the world: those who know they're in sales and those who don't. Parents are in sales. Managers are in sales. Spouses, teachers, ministers, doctors, lawyers, everybody is in sales.

Managers who learn and use the principles in this book find themselves working more effectively with less effort. They also find that, by stimulating new concepts out of what appeared to be staid employees, the quality and productivity of their subordinates increases as well.

If you're a parent and you want your children to do something, you can tell them or you can sell them. If you tell them they may do it obediently, probably grudgingly, and therefore minimally. Sell them on the idea and they'll do it enthusiastically, willingly and thoroughly. If you use the principles in this book, parenting will be easier for you, I promise.

There's a process to asking questions. It involves comprehending what happens when you ask, and what happens when someone hears. For example, when you understand that people will unintentionally give erroneous answers to your questions, you'll know how to handle that situation. When you can anticipate how someone will react to a particular type of question, you'll be able to control the interaction. You'll see how many times we predetermine the questions people ask us, and how frequently we offer meaningless responses. You'll learn how to formulate questions that will get the information you need so you can attain the things you want.

Remember, the concept is easy, the process is complicated. There is a story about the first computer, programmed in the 1950s, to assist traders on Wall Street. All the information about the stock market and how it performed was loaded into the computer. The machine, sluggish by today's standards, lumbered along for some time before sending a message to the clumsy impact printer. Traders watched anxiously as the printer tediously printed out every letter. Each of them wanted to be the first to take advantage of a high-tech tool for creating fortunes. After carefully analyzing all of the information, the computer gave the following guidelines: "Buy low, sell high."

Any trader will tell you that's the essence of the market, and that a little knowledge on Wall Street is a quick way to go broke. It's the same with the essence of the process that changed my life. It should carry a warning label, "Attempted Use Without the Proper Techniques Can Be Hazardous."

The Story Continues . . .

At the Atlanta airport, Bruce dropped Amy off at the curb. After checking her bags with the skycap, Amy turned back to him. "Now, tell me again when you'll be back in New York."

Bruce said, "There is a meeting here tomorrow. Then I'll be in Raleigh on Tuesday, and on Wednesday and Thursday I'll be in D.C. I'll be back at the apartment before rush hour on Friday."

"I'll take Friday off, spruce up the place, fix your favorite dinner and have a 'surprise' waiting for you." She gave Bruce a quick kiss, turned and headed into the terminal.

Back in Clarkesville, Claude spent a sleepless night asking himself questions. Why was Bruce so successful? Was it luck? Intelligence? Claude had made up his mind. He would go to New York and become at least half as successful as his cousin.

That evening, Claude sat in front of the television as he usually did. There was not much else to do that didn't cost money and wouldn't get him in trouble. He followed the same routine every day, even for watching television. He always sat in the same chair, with a can of soda, and always watched the same programs.

Tonight Claude's mind was not focused on the screen. He was still wondering about his cousin. It lingered on his mind all evening and was the first thing he thought of when he woke up the following morning.

Claude had been working odd jobs and part-time assignments, but this Monday morning he had nothing to do and no place to go. He followed his morning routine anyway, and walked into Annie's Cafe around seven thirty. The usual crowd was there and Claude took his usual seat.

By nine o'clock, the crowd had thinned out and Claude couldn't drink any more coffee. It was already warm outside and Claude wondered how he would use his "day off." He took stock of his assets and found he had just over $400 in his pocket. Therefore, his net worth at that moment was about $400, $650 if he added in the value of his car.

He began going through what needed to be paid. His rent was not due for a few more days but his car insurance, which the state required, had to be paid. Claude made payments weekly because he never seemed to have enough at any one time to pay things monthly.

He drove up and down Clarkesville's Main Street, looking for the best price for gas. Once he found it, he pulled his car up next to the pump and began filling the tank. As he removed the gas cap he wondered what it would be like to put gas in a car like Bruce's instead of this old clunker.

Then, for a couple of hours, he drove around the mountains thinking about his life and what he wanted to become. As he drove he passed some of the people he had known all his life. Mr. Williams was selling produce from the back of his pickup truck, which was parked under a huge tree beside the First National Bank. For as long as Claude could remember, Mr. Williams had been selling produce under that tree. The only thing that had changed in twenty years was the truck, and it had only changed once.

The more he drove, the more he realized how little things had changed. The same crops were being planted in the same fields by the same people. Most of the businesses looked the same and were run by the same people who had always run them. The problem, he decided, was this town. The sooner he could leave, the sooner he would start becoming successful.

As lunchtime approached, Claude drove toward the town square. He parked his car in front of Larry Smith's

Insurance Agency, got out and put two dimes in the parking meter. That would give him enough time to pay his insurance and eat a sandwich at Mike's Subs. The sidewalk was empty and quiet, a few cars drove slowly through the square. It was another hot, sleepy day in Clarkesville.

Once Claude stepped inside the door of Larry's agency, it was like entering a different world. The long, narrow room had once been a men's hat store, but now it had four desks along each side, all facing the front door. At the first two desks, secretaries were busily working at computers. A couple of men and a young woman were sitting at some of the other desks, either talking on the phone or writing. Claude was impressed by the activity.

At the back desk, Larry was on the telephone. He looked up, saw Claude, smiled broadly and waved. About that time one of the secretaries, Linda Sanders, turned from her computer and said, "Hi, Claude. I like that shirt. The color looks good on you."

Linda always had something nice to say. Every time Claude came in, she always stopped and greeted him. They had known each other since the first grade. Linda began making out a receipt before Claude even took out his wallet.

Larry ended his telephone call, stood up and walked toward Claude. He still had that broad grin on his face. "How's it going, Claude?"

"OK, I reckon." Claude had just spent the entire morning thinking about how rotten his life was, and he was not really sure how to answer.

Larry looked at him for a minute without saying anything and then turned to Linda. "Claude and I are going to lunch. I think I'll need another red loose leaf binder."

"There's one on the cabinet," Linda said and smiled.

Larry ushered Claude out to the sidewalk and said, "How does The Inn sound? My treat."

"Well, uh, great. Sure." Claude had not eaten at The Inn in nearly a year. For him it was a special occasion place. He couldn't imagine just having lunch on the spur of the moment at The Inn.

"It's such a pretty day, let's walk. Do you mind?" by the time Larry had finished the question he was already a step ahead of Claude. Claude found that he had to walk faster than he was accustomed to just to stay up with the man, who was twenty years older.

All the way to The Inn, Larry asked questions about what Claude enjoyed doing and what he wanted to do with his life. Once inside The Inn, the hostess saw Larry and said, "Two today, Larry? Who's your friend?"

"Yes, Ginny. This is Claude Thompson, a great client. Treat him well! What's special today?"

"Try the meat loaf, it's wonderful." Ginny's voice became more animated as she walked the two men to a window table.

Claude felt out of place and was happy that Linda had complimented his clothes that morning. It made him feel more confident.

Over lunch the questions continued. Larry asked Claude more and more specific questions about what Claude wanted to accomplish. Finally, Claude told him how Bruce's visit had caused Claude to start thinking about his own life.

"Did it start you thinking or did it just bring your thinking to a boil?" Larry asked the question and then began sipping his iced tea.

"I guess you're right, Larry. There's been a fire under that kettle for a long time. How did you know?"

"I've been there, Claude. All of us have. Are you ready to learn the secrets to real success?"

"You know, Larry, I think I am."

"Good, I thought so. When we get back to my office I'm going to give you a book to read . . ."

Claude interrupted him. "I don't know, Larry. I've never been very good at book learnin'. . . ."

"Me either," Larry had that broad grin of his again. "Claude, do you know what dyslexia is?"

"Not really."

"It's a learning disability. I have it and when I was in school the teachers thought I was lazy or stupid. They didn't know much about it then. All my life I was told that I'd never amount to anything, and I almost bought it until I found this book." Larry could tell he had struck a chord with Claude.

Larry continued, "Now, I have a hard time sitting down and reading a book, but this one's different. It's a loose leaf binder with a lot of different pages in it. Every line on every page is worth it's weight in gold. Next to the Bible, it's the most important book I have.

"I was introduced to the red book several years ago. It's produced by a group of people, most of whom I've never met, some of whom have learning disabilities like dyslexia, and some of whom don't. Whenever any of us struggles through reading a book or taking a course of some kind, we write down the most important ideas we learned on a piece of paper. Once that sheet of paper is covered with ideas, we make copies of it and send them to everyone who has a red book. Whenever we give a red book to someone, we take responsibility for making sure that they get copies as well. It takes some of the people years to fill a page with ideas that are good enough to be included. What do you think?"

Claude shook his head. "I can't believe school came that hard for you. Look at you. You have your own business, people working for you, you have a nice house and a beautiful family . . . you have two Cadillacs!"

Larry smiled. "You can have that and more, Claude."

"Yeah, I know. That's why I want to go to the city like Bruce did. There's nothin' here." As soon as he said it, Claude knew it was wrong. Just moments before he had acknowledged how successful Larry had been right there in Clarkesville.

"You need to begin reading the book, Claude. The first thing it will teach you is that success is not out there somewhere, it's here, here and here." As Larry spoke he pointed to his heart, his head and his hand. "Soul, mind and body, Claude. Remember that, soul, mind and body.

"Those three are constantly talking to each other. Your soul, your spirit, your attitude can determine how your mind thinks and how your body feels. Your mind can convince your body that it is well or ill, and it can make or break your spirit. A healthy, active body keeps the mind thinking and the spirit soaring.

"Soul, mind and body, Claude. That's the first lesson." Larry looked at a silent Claude, smiled and pointed to his heart, his head and his hand.

Back in Larry's office, Claude took the red book as if it was made of glass. As Larry walked him to the door he said, "If you think you need to go to the city, you go. It can't hurt, and you'll certainly learn a lot."

Claude thanked Larry again and went over to his car. He felt a tap on his shoulder, turned and saw Linda standing there with a receipt. "Isn't this what you came for?" she asked.

"Oh, yeah, I forgot." Claude reached into his wallet and pulled out a twenty dollar bill. "Here," he said.

"And here's your receipt, Mr. Thompson. You're quite fortunate, you know. Larry has only given out three red books. He must think a lot of you." Linda turned and went back into the store-front office.

Claude looked back through the plate glass window and saw that Larry was already on the telephone, smiling broadly. Claude picked up the red book and opened it. The first page was a photocopy of what was apparently an old document. It was handwritten and smudged, but still readable. The page contained about twenty short statements. Claude had no idea what those statements meant, nor was he aware of how they would affect him. All he could think about was that he was going to make something out of his life like Bruce and Larry had done with theirs.

"My mind's made up," Claude said to no one, and he backed his car away from the curb.

CHAPTER TWO

Taking Control

Has this ever happened to you?

You're walking down the hall and someone is walking toward you. Typically, you say, "How are you?"

The other person responds, "Fine."

Then the other person asks, "How are you?" And you say, "Fine."

Have you ever tried saying something else? Try saying something like, "I'm having a great day," and you'll probably hear something like, "You've been reading too many of those motivational books." Or, if you say, "Well, now that you asked, I really don't feel all that well," the response may be, "Look, you've got your problems, I've got mine."

This happens many times every week to most of us. In fact, *most* questioning is done out of habit, and that's why it isn't effective.

The Routine Question

Too often we ask and are asked questions that demand no answer, because the question is used as a simple form of small-talk communication.

Recently I had the following telephone conversation:

"Marge! It's Chuck! How are you?"

"Fine, thanks."

"I'm fine, thanks. Is DuPree around?"

Notice that I answered a question Marge didn't ask. Because we are so conditioned to respond to certain stimuli in certain ways, I fell into the trap even as I was writing a book on effective questioning techniques.

If we have been conditioned to ask questions we don't want answered, and to give answers that have no relevance to reality, is it any wonder that we have not been taking full advantage of the possibilities effective questioning could offer?

Try taking control by being aware of your questions and answers for one week and see what a difference it can make. To do that, you must first understand the power and impact of the basic types of questions—who, what, where, why, and when. If we take a closer look at each, we can determine how we have conditioned our minds to react and respond to them. Just as we have programmed ourselves to go through the "How are you/ Fine/How are you" scenario without thinking, registering or remembering it, we have also programmed our minds to trigger certain responses to other types of questions.

I'll use an example to explain what I mean. Read the following sentence and count the number of times the letter "F" appears in the sentence.

> Finished files are the result of years of scientific study combined with the knowledge of many years of experts

How many did you find? If you are like most people who see this for the first time, you saw three of them. Maybe you saw five or even six. Actually, there are seven, and if you missed any, they were probably the "Fs" in the words "of."

This exercise has been around for a long time, and many of us have been using it for years. Yet even the people who have seen it before will only see three "Fs," because our minds have been conditioned to think in a certain way. To understand this completely we have to look at how we were taught.

Back in the first grade when we were learning the alphabet, the teacher taught us that the letters were sounds or phonetic devices, not shapes or symbols. When most people see this exercise for the first time, the subconscious mind takes over and begins seeking a sound, not a shape. Since the "Fs" in the word "of" have the wrong sound, the subconscious mind tends to reject them as "Fs".

Similar conditioning has been taking place all of our lives. We learn not only to ask and answer questions in certain ways, we're cautioned that asking questions will tell the world how little we know.

TIP #3

Asking Is A Sign of Wisdom, Not Ignorance

"Who" Questions are often perceived as accusatory. Your earliest recollection of a "who" question might be an adult standing over some mess and asking the dreaded, "Who did this?" When you read the question, was the first answer to pop in your mind, "Not me?" Even as adults, the "who" question is deemed an accusation, subconsciously if not consciously. After all, when your history teacher asked a "who" question, you were expected to know the right answer. If you cannot recall a specific incident, there is probably one embedded in your subconscious mind that instantly caused you to begin formulating a "Not me!" response.

The story is told of the little boy who was sitting in his fourth grade class when the teacher asked, "Who shot Lincoln?" His immediate response was, "Not me. Besides it was a Chrysler, not a Lincoln, and my BB gun won't shoot that far."

Whenever you ask a "who" question, understand that the person being asked will not be able to avoid an initial "Not me" reaction. After years of conditioning, we can cause our conscious response to be less defensive, but our initial *reaction* will still be "Not me".

Ask a child a "who" question and the child literally will respond, "Not me!" Ask teenagers and they will pause for a moment and give the universal teenage response,

"Idunno." During that pause, at the mind's lightening speed, they went through the following thought process: "She thinks I did that. I'm always getting blamed for everything around here. It's not fair. Hey, everybody's supposed to be innocent until proven guilty. Wait a minute, maybe I did do it. Let me see. Nah, I don't think so. Besides, how important can it be? Adults are so up-tight. It doesn't matter." That entire thought process is summed up in "Idunno."

The whole thinking process for the teenager took less than a nanosecond, one millionth of a second. When we ask a question, the mind is kicked into gear. People mentally retrieve and sort through a massive amount of information.

When we reach adulthood, we have had more experience with the "who" questions and although our initial reaction is still, "Not me," the way we respond is usually more refined and comes after a longer pause. Remember this the next time you want to ask a "who" question. Understand that the thought process natural to us all is going to distort the response.

You can avoid this pitfall by avoiding "who" questions. That is, don't put the "who" at the beginning of the question and, if you can, leave it off entirely. If you need to know who is responsible for something, use an "if" question. For instance, you could say, "If I wanted to know the person responsible for billing errors, where would I look?"

What's the difference? An "if" question is always open to speculation. "If" questions do not ask for commitment and they leave a way out. They are much softer questions than the tougher "who" questions.

Another way to soft pedal the "who" question is to phrase it as an opinion question. "Who would you say is ultimately responsible for customer service?" is a much more digestible way of asking. When a person answers, "I am" to a "who would you say ..." question, they are accepting responsibility. When the same person answers, "I am" to a "who" question, they are accepting guilt. The distinction between the two forms can make a critical difference in the depth and accuracy of the answer you receive.

"What" Questions are some of the most powerful questions around. These are used to solicit factual or speculative information. Compare "What state has the most boats per capita?" to "What state would you think has the most boats per capita?" The answer to the first question will give us accurate information about the number of boats, the second will give us the opinion of the person answering the question. Later on you will see how certain "what" questions can bring you information you never thought available.

"Where" Questions solicit information and are typically non-threatening. Any time we ask someone else for information we are sending a subliminal message that we think they know something we don't. Usually, this is a positive message, and usually it is true. Making someone else an authority, letting them know that we think they know more than we, elevates our image in their minds and makes them feel important. I say usually, because when we ask someone where our sunglasses are and they say, "On your head," we do little to enhance our image. However, we position people as "the authority" when we ask for directions or where a certain department is. Let's face it, we all like to be an authority once in while.

Nevertheless, we can't be the authority all the time. *Wisdom* is knowing what we don't know, and being willing to ask about it. *Ignorance* is being unaware that we don't know. *Stubbornness* is understanding that we don't know and still not asking.

Anytime you can rephrase a threatening question and make it a non-threatening one, do it. When you can change a "who" question to a "where" question, you will usually receive better information.

"Why" Questions are the single most threatening questions, and anytime we use the words "why" and "you" in the same question, we will trigger the strongest subliminal reaction possible. That's because the "Why did you/ Why do you . . ." question mentally challenges a person's decisions, actions and self-esteem. It puts up for scrutiny whatever someone has done and the reason for doing it. None of us likes that very much.

To avoid the "why" question, and even the "why/you" combination, try using the less-threatening "where" and "what" questions. Instead of, "Why did you do that?" try, "Where did you learn how to do that?" Instead of, "Why do you act that way?" try something like, "What kind of response do you think that approach elicits?" or, "When do you think that type of behavior is most/least effective?" See the difference?

Instead of challenging people and forcing them to defend their positions, we are softening the question and causing them to think. We may still expect them to justify their actions, but the way the question is phrased leaves communication open and permits unrestrained dialogue.

Whenever you find yourself wanting to ask a "why" question, stop. As you think about rephrasing the question you will also find yourself thinking about what you really want to know. In a later section you will see how beneficial this can be.

"When" Questions are a lot like "where" questions in that they position the person being asked as an authority. They typically cause the answerer to delay in responding, and they solicit a new view of the issue.

Salespeople know that the "when" question is a great one for closing. For instance, "When would you like us to deliver this?" and, "When were you planning your move to this area?"

You can frequently elicit more specific answers using "when" questions, because they are easier to answer. "When would you like to go to lunch?" is easier than "Where would you like to eat?" and "When can we expect a decision?" is easier than "What is your decision?"

"How" Questions create a little more pressure than "when" and "where" questions, because the person being questioned may feel the stress of having to come up with the "right" answer. If we are looking for ideas about how to accomplish a certain task, we must to be sure that's what we communicate, and that we avoid appearing to put people "on the spot."

Question softeners can be effective here, too. Try a combination of "how" and "would": "How would you say . . ." and "How would you suggest. . . ." These are much less threatening than, "How do you plan to do that?"

Effective Questioning begins with knowing what you want to learn, determining who has the information, and what it would take to get that person to tell you. The final step is to create the scenario that will cause them to give you the most valuable answer possible.

TIP #5

If You're Goal Is to Win a Battle of Wits, Or to Be Viewed as An Authority, You May Have to Settle for Less Information

---

Robert Woodruff ran the Coca-Cola company for many years and was an admired and respected businessman. He is credited with saying, "It's amazing what you can accomplish when you don't care who gets the credit." In intelligent questioning, it's amazing what you can learn when you don't care who gets the temporary position of authority.

In working with parents who are having difficulty communicating with their children, I usually find that the lack of communication has its roots in the questions they exchange. The parents are usually asking a lot of "why/you" questions which their offspring resent, and the children are asking a lot of "Why me?" questions which the parents ignore. In a later chapter we will talk about the impact that inflection and phrasing can have on questions. However, your questions can be softened considerably by using the techniques we've already discussed. Not only will your rapport with your kids improve, your family life and your blood pressure will also improve, and it's a good way to practice the questioning techniques you will want to use on the job.

Who, what, where, why, when questions can be the building blocks for more meaningful interactions. Just remember when to ask a who question, who to ask a what question, where to ask a when question and how to ask the right questions.

Any questions?

The Story Continues . . .

It had been a month since the reunion. Bruce and Amy were spending their Thursday night as they always did, at Bruce's apartment. To the soft background of jazz on the CD player, they prepared dinner and drank a glass of their favorite wine. Then they ate at the small table near the living room window, and discussed their plans for the weekend.

While Bruce's apartment was not prestigious, the neighborhood was. The living room was barely large enough for a sofa, a chair and the table at the window where most of the meals were eaten. The kitchen was about the size of a large closet, but it had a remarkable amount of storage space. The bedroom was the largest room, so Bruce kept his stereo there, along with a large rack to hold the clothes that would not fit in his closet.

After dinner, the couple sat on the sofa enjoying the evening. They were interrupted by the ringing of the telephone. Bruce looked at the clock. It was after ten. He picked up the phone and heard a too-familiar voice.

"How's it goin', Cuz?"

Bruce was hoping he was having a dream. He wasn't. "Claude. What a pleasant surprise." His mind was racing. The only reason Claude would be calling was to say he was planning to visit. Bruce had to think of ways to discourage Claude from coming to New York, and he had to think quickly.

"How's everything in Clarkesville?" Bruce was stalling for time.

"It'us fine when I left. I'm here!"

"You're where?" Bruce's voice was shaking and Amy's face was falling.

"LaGuardia! How 'bout that?" Claude knew his cousin

would be surprised, but he underestimated how surprised Bruce would be.

Before Bruce could say anything Claude continued. "Just tell me how to get to your place from here and I'll be there directly."

"Uh, Claude, why didn't you tell me you were coming?" Bruce looked at Amy in time to catch the look of annoyance that came across her face.

"I wanted to surprise you. Besides, I just decided yesterday that there was no time like the present. Now, which way is your place from here?" Claude was looking around the airport as he talked on the pay phone.

"Well, you can take the train or you can come by taxi. You could take one of the shuttle services to a hotel and then take a taxi on over here. Actually, that would be best. The trains don't run very often this time of night and it could be confusing for you. A taxi will cost you about forty dollars from the air . . ."

"FORTY DOLLARS!" Claude could not believe his ears. Who would pay that kind of money for a taxi ride? Just a few taxi rides like that would buy Claude another car like the one he had in Clarkesville.

Bruce continue, "So the best way is to take the hotel shuttle to the Hyatt . . . no, wait a minute, there are two Hyatt Hotels. Let's see. Take the shuttle to the Waldorf, can you remember that? The Waldorf?"

"I think so." There was a little uncertainty in Claude's voice.

"OK. When you get to the Waldorf, find a taxi and give the driver this address: one fifty-six East Fifth Street. Got it?"

"One fifty-six Fifth Street. Right." Claude had nothing to write on so he was trying to commit everything to memory.

"EAST Fifth Street."

"Oh. One fifty-six *East* Fifth Street." Claude was nodding.

"When you get to the building, come into the foyer and ring up for me." Bruce was thinking about how and where he would accommodate his unexpected guest.

"Bruce, how do I 'ring up for you?'"

Bruce had forgotten how strange the city had been to him when he first arrived. "On the wall in the foyer you will see a panel with a lot of doorbells. Beside the third one from the top on the right you'll see my name. Push that button. It'll ring a bell here in the apartment and I'll come down and help you in.

Claude was unsure whether he could pull this off, but he was willing to try. After all, he had come to the city to be successful. "OK. One more thing, Bruce. What's a foyer?"

Bruce was beginning to think that maybe he should drive out to LaGuardia and pick up his cousin. He was beginning to remember how it felt to be in the city for the first time. Even though he had been far more sophisticated when he came to New York than Claude would ever be, it was still unnerving to deal with the ways of a big city.

Bruce turned around to speak to Amy. He was surprised to see that she was already wearing her coat. Bruce spoke into the phone, "Hold on a second, Claude."

Amy spoke first. "It sounds like you'll have a different houseguest tonight."

"Look, he's my cousin. It'll only be for one night and it's too late to try a hotel. Besides he probably doesn't have the money for a decent room. Ride with me to pick him up and we can continue to plan our weekend."

"No thanks," Amy said, "I've had enough of your Hicksville relatives for awhile." She kissed Bruce on the cheek and opened the door. "See you tomorrow," she said. She wasn't smiling.

Bruce went back to the telephone. "Are you still there, Claude?"

"Yeah, Cuz."

"Which airline did you fly in on?"

"You mean like United or American?"

"Yes, Claude, which one?"

"Delta."

"Are you still at the baggage claim area?"

"I'm not sure what that is." Claude was looking around again.

"It's where you picked up your luggage. Are you still down where you picked up your suitcases?"

"Heck no, Bruce, I got my luggage at Wal-Mart before I left Clarkesville."

"You didn't check your bags?" Bruce was beginning to wonder if he could find his cousin even if he did go to LaGuardia.

"Well, I made sure the zippers worked and the strap was there and it wasn't torn or anything. But usually you can trust Wal-Mart."

"Bruce realized that, while they were both speaking English, they were talking different languages.

"Claude, listen closely. I'm going to drive out and get you. It will take me about forty-five minutes, so here's what I want you to do. Go get a cup of coffee or something and then meet me at the Delta ticket counter in forty-five minutes. The Delta ticket counter, got it? Can you do that?"

Claude thought a minute and then answered, "Sure. But I hate to make you come out this late."

"Believe me, Claude, it's the easiest way."

Within an hour the two men were walking out to the curb where Bruce had parked his car. It was a BMW convertible but it was black instead of the red one he'd been driving at the reunion.

Claude looked at the car for a minute and said, "How many of these do you have?"

"Just one, why?" Bruce said.

"Well, 'cause last time you'us drivin' a red one."

"That was a rental, Claude. I flew into Atlanta and rented that one," Bruce explained. "This one is mine."

As they drove, Bruce pointed out several major buildings on the skyline. Claude seemed more and more overwhelmed and Bruce began to relive his first days in New York. Showing the city to his cousin gave Bruce a renewed appreciation for the exciting environment in which he lived.

Riding through the downtown streets, Claude began to wonder if he had made the right decision. New York was much larger than he had imagined. Street after street appeared and, before long, all the streets and all the buildings began to look alike.

Finally they reached Bruce's apartment building and drove up to a huge steel door that was closed. Bruce lowered the car's power window, and entered a five-digit number into the key pad on top of a metal pole. The door opened, Bruce drove in and the door closed immediately behind them.

Bruce backed the BMW into his parking space and said, "This is home, Claude." Bruce got out taking Claude's two bags with him. The suitcases were much smaller than what Bruce would have brought. He hoped it meant that Claude was not planning a long stay.

Claude followed Bruce to the elevator and looked around. "Where's the button?" Claude asked.

"There isn't one. It uses a key, see?" Bruce inserted a key into the slot in the wall panel and the elevator door opened. The two men stepped in, Bruce inserted the key into a slot beside the lamp labeled "5," and the elevator began to move.

Bruce noticed that his cousin had become unusually quiet. "It's pretty tight security, isn't it?"

"Like Fort Knox!" Claude said.

When they stepped off the elevator on the fifth floor, Claude was amazed to see that so many people could live all jammed up together. Both sides of the hall were lined with doors, a lot like the hotel on his one trip to Atlanta. He noticed that the doors had three, sometimes four locks on them.

They stopped at apartment 521. Using three separate keys, Bruce unlocked his door and opened it. Claude was thinking that these must be fabulous apartments since they required such extensive security. He was disappointed when he walked in and saw how small it was but, being a Southern Gentleman, he didn't make any comment.

"Hope you don't mind the sofa, Claude." Bruce put the bags he was carrying on the floor at the end of the sofa.

"Not at all, Cuz. I really appreciate you puttin' me up tonight. I'll find a place tomorrow."

"Want some coffee?" Bruce was already in the kitchen when he asked.

"That'd be great."

Bruce took some coffee beans out of the refrigerator and poured them into the grinder. Then he took a triangular filter out of a drawer and put it in the coffee maker. Claude just watched and said nothing. A few minutes later the two men were at the table by the window talking about their days in Clarkesville. The longer they talked, the more animated the conversation became.

The coffee ran out, so Bruce made another pot. It was nearly three a.m. when they finally decided to call it a night. They continued to talk as Claude spread sheets over the sofa and Bruce brought him towels.

In the dark and quiet, both men were thinking about the differences between Clarkesville and New York, about how much each of them had changed in the past few years, and about how alike they still were in so many ways. After awhile their thoughts diverged, Bruce thinking about how successful he had been, and Claude thinking about how successful he would become.

The next morning Bruce's clock rang as usual at six a.m. The short sleep had left him groggy. He sat up, decided he would shower and then wake his cousin. Then he noticed the aroma of coffee in the apartment.

"Mornin', Cuz." Claude handed Bruce a cup of coffee while Bruce sat in bed. "Your coffee makin' system is a might complicated, but it sure beats instant, don't it?"

Bruce noticed that Claude had already showered, shaved and dressed. "How long have you been up?"

"I'us too excited to sleep. I studied your newspaper, lookin' for jobs and a place to stay. I think I'm gonna need your help decidin' where's the best place to live."

"Right. Tell you what, let me get going and we'll talk." Bruce took a sip of coffee and headed for the shower. When he was dressed, he stepped back into the living room. Claude had put away all of his belongings as well as the sheets he had slept on. In fact, Bruce thought, the place had never looked better. He found Claude in the kitchen.

"Hope you don't mind, Cuz," Claude said. He was holding two eggs in his hands, "I'm makin' us a little breakfast. Still like your eggs sunny side up?"

"Well, I guess so. I haven't been eating eggs much lately. Amy knows a lot about nutrition and she says the cholesterol in eggs is bad for you." Then Bruce smiled and said, "But, what the heck. Two can't hurt."

As the men ate, Bruce said, "There's no way I can skip work today, Claude. We have a major review of our marketing plan at nine. It'll probably last all day."

"No problem, Cuz," Claude said, "I'm gonna run out and find me a job and see 'bout an apartment."

"Uh, Claude, it may not be as easy here as it was in Clarkesville to find a job, and finding an apartment will be virtually impossible. Why do you want to be in New York?"

"My mind's made up, Bruce. It's that simple. Besides, with all these buildings around here there must be hundreds of apartments and thousands of jobs."

Bruce was putting his dishes in the sink. "Claude, if there was an opening at Genre, I'd find a way to put you in it. As for an apartment, well it took us over three years to find this place. Wow, look at the time!"

With a few parting words, Bruce was out the door.

Later, when Claude stepped out onto the sidewalk, the sun was finding it's way between the tall buildings. To keep from getting lost, Claude planned to walk in an ever-widening circle. He would check out the businesses and the apartment buildings in Bruce's neighborhood.

After about an hour of dodging the cars and pedestrians, Claude began to notice that most of the businesses seemed to be small stores and shops just like the ones in Clarkesville. He was not fully aware that the tall buildings were filled with every type of vocation and profession. Claude only saw what was at eye level.

Around ten o'clock the stores began opening and Claude started going in and asking for a job. In virtually every store, Claude was given a curt response and handed an application. He filled out all the forms, giving Bruce's address and telephone number.

It was nearly one in the afternoon when Claude decided to stop for lunch. He took the only vacant stool at the lunch counter and sat between two men, one who looked like a young executive, the other a seasoned salesman. In Clarkesville it was customary to chat with the others at the lunch counter, even if they were strangers.

After ordering, Claude turned to the young man on his left and asked if he knew Bruce Thompson. Claude figured that since they dressed alike they probably worked in the same place. The young man was more interested in avoiding conversation than in being polite. After several false starts, Claude heard a voice say, "Where are you from?"

He turned to his right and saw the older salesman smiling at him.

"Clarkesville. Clarkesville, Georgia. How 'bout you?"

"New York. Actually, I came here from Pittsburgh, but that was so long ago it seems like I've always lived here. But I wouldn't live anywhere else."

"Why?"

"I don't know, really. Maybe it's the excitement and the opportunity the city offers. Maybe it's the people. You know, some of the finest people in the world live here, uh . . . I don't know your name. I'm Alan Cimberg," the man said, extending his hand.

Claude shook his hand. "Claude Thompson."

"What brings you to New York, Claude?"

"I came to be successful like my cousin Bruce."

"What does 'successful' mean to you, Claude?"

"Well, Bruce drives a BMW, lives in a nice apartment, wears good clothes, and has a great-looking girlfriend."

"Is that your idea of success or your cousin's?" Alan was smiling as if he was enjoying the conversation immensely.

"Oh. I never thought 'bout that."

"Do you think it might be a good idea to decide what success is before you go looking for it?" Alan asked.

"Yeah. Good idea."

"Maybe I can help. What do you enjoy doing? What's fun for you, Claude?"

"Well, fishin' and huntin'. I like drivin' around and I think drivin' Bruce's BMW would be great!"

"Wouldn't driving your own BMW be better?"

"Yeah, no kiddin'."

"Now let me ask you this, Claude, and think about it before you answer. What have you done that gave you the greatest sense of pride and accomplishment?"

Claude thought for a moment and then responded, "Well, I guess I'd have to say the times I helped somebody out. You know, like when you help someone who can't help themselves. There's this one lady in Clarkesville who lives alone and she's kinda' feeble. Every now and again I go by her place and fix faucets, or replace burned-out light bulbs, or clean up her yard. It always leaves me feelin' good. Is that what you mean?"

"That's it. Whatever gives us a sense of fulfillment is what success is for us."

"But you can't make a livin' out of heppin' people."

"Actually, Claude, helping people is the only way I've found to be successful."

"You mean you can get paid for heppin' others?"

"Handsomely."

"And that's what you do?"

"I'm glad you asked that question. I'm a motivational speaker. I stand up in front of crowds and give them ideas they can use to be more successful. I help people become better at whatever they're trying to accomplish with their lives. Perhaps I can help you. What would you like to know?"

Claude was taken aback. He wasn't sure what question he should ask, although he felt he should ask *something*. After a long pause, Alan spoke again. "I must be on my way, but I'll leave you with something another motivational speaker once said. *'You can have anything you want if you do two things: help enough other people to have what they want, and learn how to ask for what you want.'*"

With that, Alan was gone.

"Will there be anything else?" The man behind the counter was interrupting Claude's deepest thoughts.

"Sorry, what'd you say?"

"You want anything else?"

"No, just the check, please."

Alan's words were still swimming in Claude's mind as he walked up Eighth Street. "You can have anything you want if you *help*. . . . Helping people is the only way I've found to be successful." That's when Claude saw the little sign, HELP WANTED.

Inside the small shop Claude was surrounded by more T-shirts and sweatshirts than he had ever seen. Most had New York things on them, such as outlines of the skyline. Behind the counter where the cash register stood was a young woman who was chewing gum and thumbing through a magazine. When Claude walked up to the counter she spoke without ever taking her eyes off the page.

"May I help you?"

"Yeah. I'm here to hep."

This unexpected response caused her to look up, but it did not break her gum-chewing rhythm. She was not like the girls in Clarkesville. There weren't any girls there who would wear multi-colored hair, leather everything and nearly a dozen earrings.

"You what?"

"I'm here to hep. Your sign . . .," Claude was pointing to the sign in the window but he couldn't take his eyes off the sight in front of him. "Your sign says ya' want some hep."

She gazed at Claude for a minute as if he were a Martian, and yelled at the top of her lungs, Bill!" then she went back to her magazine as Claude continued to stare.

From the back room came a young man, a little older than Claude. He looked in Claude's direction and said, "What is it?"

Since the young woman was absorbed in her studies, Claude spoke. "I'm here 'bout your sign."

"What sign . . . oh, yeah." The sign had been in the window for so long that the young man had forgotten about it. "Are you looking for a job?"

"Reckon so. What kinda' hep do ya' need?

"Where are you from?"

"Clarkesville. Clarkesville, Georgia. Ever been there?"

"Uh, no. My name's Bill." With that he extended his hand.

"Claude Thompson. What do y'all do 'round here, anyway?"

"We sell T-shirts, sweatshirts and other trinkets, mostly to tourists who come in for souvenirs. Have you ever worked in retail before?"

"At the lumber yard back in Clarkesville I worked out front some. Mostly I sold lumber and tools, ya' know."

"Well, I need a stock boy who can sort out the merchandise as it comes in, keep the shelves stocked and pick up around the store. Think you can do that?"

"Well, show me where the things come in and how ya' sort them and I'll tell ya'."

After a few minutes in the back room and a quick tour of the store, Claude felt comfortable with the job. Remembering what he had learned at lunch, he decided to ask for what he wanted. He thought for a minute and then said, "I can hep ya', Bill. Now I need a salary."

Bill was smiling. He'd had a few inquiries for the job, but this was the strangest interview ever. "It pays six dollars an hour to start, forty hours a week, fifty-cent raises every six months if you work out. When can you start?"

"Now. Actually, I need to go look for an apartment this afternoon, how 'bout first thing in the mornin'?"

"You're kidding, right?" Bill stared at his new employee and continued. "No, you aren't. How long have you been in New York, Claude?"

"Since yesterday. Why?"

"Do you have a place to stay?"

"Oh yeah, I'm stayin' with my cousin a few blocks from here."

"It may take you awhile to find a place to live, and when you do it'll be very expensive."

"You sound just like my cousin. All you New York folks sure look at the gloomy side of things, don't ya'? What time do ya' want me here?"

"Nine o'clock, we open at ten. Angela will be here." Bill paused a minute and added, "Probably."

The sun was hot on Claude's face as he walked the streets in the neighborhood around NY/NY, the shop where his fortune would begin. He wanted to find an apartment nearby and was sure that Bruce had been wrong about the difficulty of finding one. Perhaps Bruce had not looked hard enough.

However, after visiting nearly twenty buildings and being told, by increasingly rude landlords, that there were only waiting lists, Claude was about to concede defeat. Then something caught his eye: a window with no curtains or shades.

The apartment building was less than two blocks from the store. Claude could see through the window that the basement unit was empty. He went up the steps and looked at the rows of doorbell buttons. Most of the name tags were so worn that they were hard to read, but Claude found the one that he thought said "Manager" and pushed the button.

The small speaker crackled and soon a curt voice said, "We ain't buyin'!"

Claude was amused. "I'm here 'bout the apartment. I need to rent it."

"We don't have any vacancies. Go away."

"What 'bout the one y'all got downstairs?"

There was a long pause. Then the voice asked, "Where are you from?"

"Clarkesville. Clarkesville, Georgia."

"I'll be damned . . . wait right there."

In a few minutes a short, rotund woman appeared at the door and looked at Claude. "What's your name?"

"Claude Thompson."

"No, I thought you were somebody else. I grew up in Helen. Used to go to Clarkesville once in awhile to see a movie. It's a small world, ain't it?"

"Yeah. Been back to Helen lately? It's real nice, got lots of shops, and tourists come in there like you wouldn't believe." Claude was always more relaxed talking about back-home things.

After celebrating "old home week" on the steps of the

building for nearly thirty minutes, Claude learned that Mrs. Murphy had been in New York for more than three decades, was a widow and owned the apartment building.

"How 'bout that apartment?"

"Oh, Claude, I wish I could rent it to you. Actually, I wish I could rent it to anybody, but I can't."

"Why not?"

"It's kind of complicated. You see the unit needs a lot of work—plumbing, electrical, painting—and I can't afford to get it fixed. Actually, I can afford to but it doesn't make sense. This building's rent is controlled by the city and there's no way I would ever make my money back if I did all the work that it needs. Maybe someday the rent controls will come off and I can."

"So the apartment just sits empty?" Claude was dumb-founded.

"I'm afraid so. Good luck."

"Well, could I just *see* the place?"

"Why would you want to do that?"

"Maybe the place could be fixed up easier than you think. Whaddya have to lose?"

Mrs. Murphy thought a minute and then said, "You're right. I'll get the key."

After they went through the unit, it was clear that each of them was seeing a different apartment. Mrs. Murphy saw a damaged unit that produced no revenue. Claude saw a potentially luxurious apartment. "Look," said Claude, "the plumbin' damage here is mostly on the surface. I could fix that for ya'. Patchin' the plaster is somethin' I could do in a couple of evenings. 'Course paintin' ain't nothin', and the 'lectrical problems are really simpler than the plumbin'. Why don't ya' let me live here and fix it up?"

Mrs. Murphy wanted to believe in the simplicity of Claude's suggestion for two reasons. One was that it would give her a rentable unit, and the other was that she was beginning to like Claude.

"It's a nice thought, Claude, but it's not that simple.

You see, the city requires permits, the union people get involved, and it all becomes a very complicated matter."

"If I get the permits do we have a deal?"

Mrs. Murphy thought she had nothing to lose. Claude would try to get the permits, he'd get bogged down in red tape and she'd never hear from him again. "Sure," she said. Even though she knew there was little use, she gave Claude her address and phone number.

They shook hands. Claude was beaming. "Which way's City Hall?"

If Claude thought some of the landlords were rude, he was about to get a lesson in bureaucratic arrogance. The cab driver on the way over warned him that it would not be as easy to get things done in New York as it was in Clarkesville, and he was right. Nobody at City Hall knew who he needed to talk to or how to approach his problem.

It was nearly five o'clock when Claude realized he must have spoken to everyone in the building. People were beginning to leave and Claude was becoming disillusioned. He walked into another office, only to find all of the desks empty except one. By now the sun was casting long shadows across the floor, which made the air appear smokier than it was. At an old wooden desk in the back corner sat a man in his sixties who was reading a piece of paper. He looked up when he heard Claude come in.

"Yeah?"

"'Scuse me, I'm lookin' for someone who can tell me how to get a permit."

"A permit for what?"

"Uh, to fix up an apartment. Ya' know some light plumbin', 'lectrical, paintin', things like that."

"You have a license?"

"Yessir. Got a Georgia journeyman's license."

"That's no good here. Get a New York permit and come back."

"That'll take months. 'Sides, I only want to fix up my place, I'm not goin' into business or anything."

"You own this apartment and want a homeowner's permit?"

"Nope, gonna rent it. The lady who owns it says I can rent it if I fix it up but I need a permit." This was the longest conversation Claude had had with anyone at City Hall.

"Oh. Well, wish I could help, but the regulations won't permit it. Even to fix up one unit you need the licenses." The man could see the disappointment come across Claude's face.

"Are you sure?"

"Hey, I've been in this department nearly forty years. These young kids who work here don't know half what I know. Look," he said, waving his hand around, "by five o'clock they're all gone. No work ethic."

Claude saw a ray of hope. "Yeah, I know what you mean. I remember at the mill I used to get all the over-time I wanted 'cause other people weren't willin' to work. I just got to New York last night and I start work tomor-row, and yet there's folks on the street beggin' 'cause they can't find a job. Why is that?"

"Beats me, buddy." The man leaned back and lit a small cigar. "It's like everybody wants something for noth-ing."

"Yeah. Kinda' makes it hard for those who do want to make somethin' of themselves, don't it? Like this lady with the apartment. She's a widow, can't rent the unit, can't fix it up. People are standin' in lines 'round here for a place to live, and she's got a place nobody can live in. Strange, ain't it?"

The man puffed on his cigar for a minute, trying to decide if he was being conned or if Claude was sincere. "Where you from?"

"Clarkesville. Clarkesville, Georgia. M'name's Claude Thompson. What's yours?"

"Goodman. Shel."

Claude reached out his hand. "Nice to meet ya', Shel. You're the first person here to give me some real infor-mation. I don't 'specially 'preciate what you're tellin' me, but I do 'preciate your time."

Shel took another puff on his cigar as he looked Claude in the eyes. In a moment a large grin came across Shel's face. "Why doesn't this lady's building superintendent fix the place up?"

Claude thought for a moment and then said, "I don't think she has one."

Shel continued to smile at Claude without saying a word. Claude's mind was racing as he tried to figure out what was going on. "Buildin' superintendents don't need permits?"

"Not for what you're talking about. We would consider them routine repairs. Think this lady would hire you?"

"I'll sure ask her!" Claude looked at Shel's telephone and Shel slid it over to him.

"Mrs. Murphy? Claude. I think we've got it worked out. I'm gonna be your building superintendent so's we don't need permits. I'll fix the place up and pay, uh, I forgot to ask how much the rent would be."

There was a pause. Shel was creating a continuous stream of smoke from his cigar as he watched Claude's reaction to the conversation.

"Well, OK, I think I can handle that."

Shel spoke up. "Ask her who's gonna buy the materials you'll need."

Claude relayed Shel's question and said, "OK, you'll take care of that. Well, I guess that's it . . . wait a second, Shel wants to talk to you. Shel Goodman, he's my new friend down here at City Hall."

Claude handed the telephone to Shel and, after some cursory introductions, heard Shel say, "Yeah, he's a piece of work, all right. Look, maybe I can help you with the materials, I know a lot of people. Take this number down. . . ."

As the conversation continued Claude thought how right he'd been. New York was a place where you can have anything for which you asked.

By the time Claude got back to Bruce's apartment it was nearly seven o'clock. "Where have you been? Amy and I were worried about you. This is a tough city, Claude, you can't just roam around like you do in Clarkesville, especially at night." Bruce was both angry and relieved. Amy was obviously annoyed with the whole situation, since Claude was becoming a major disruption in her life. She wondered how long it would last.

"I had a great day, Cuz. Got a job, uh, make that two jobs but one don't pay nothin', and an apartment." Bruce and Amy were speechless. When they regained their senses they each assumed that Claude had been taken in by some con artist.

"You . . . you got a job?"

Before Claude could answer, Amy interrupted, "You found an apartment?"

"Yep. Stock boy at NY/NY, the City's finest casual 'parel store, accordin' to Bill. He's my boss." Claude was enjoying this report of his success. "Got an apartment a couple of blocks away in the buildin' where I'm the superintendent."

Claude was enjoying a little too much the fun he was having at Bruce and Amy's expense. They weren't buying it.

"Wait a minute, Claude." Bruce had to investigate this one. "One thing at a time. How much does this job pay?"

"Six dollars an hour, raises every six months, forty hours a week. Pretty good just startin' out, huh?"

"Actually, Claude, it won't go far in this city. How much does your other job pay?"

"Nothin'. My friend at City Hall said if I was the buildin' superintendent I could do the repairs on the place without a lot of permits and stuff. So, Mrs. Murphy went along with it and I'm gonna work off part of my rent."

Amy jumped in, "So this apartment is a run-down little place in a tenement house. Now that makes more sense. Is it like a cold-water, fourth floor walkup?"

Claude was not liking Amy any more than he had in Clarkesville. Her words and the tone of her voice made him think she might be trying to put him down. "No, it's basement level," said Claude, "has a couple o' windows that look out on the sidewalk. It's probably a little bigger than this apartment, but this one's much fancier. It has a water heater. . . . Look, I just went out and asked for hep. There's a lot o' people in New York, I figured some of 'em must be willin' to hep. You just gotta ask."

Bruce and Amy had the strangest looks on their faces.

"Dinner's on me," Claude said. "Tonight we're celebratin' and I'll tell you the whole story over dinner at the deli. See, I'm even startin' to sound like the New Yorker that I am."

CHAPTER THREE

How To Ask A Question

"You don't want to buy anything today, do you?"

The average person is going to say "No" to that question, but why will the answer be no?

First, most of us like to please other people. Even captains of industry, the most hard-nosed individuals, have told me privately that they really hate having to turn people down. However, when people ask us to turn them down and we think it is in our best interests to do so, the whole process becomes amazingly simple. The way this particular question is phrased, we are led to believe we are meeting the other person's expectation when we turn them down.

Second, the wording of the question places certain expectations on us. There is an anticipated pattern of action established here, and we're supposed to live up to it by declining to buy.

Now you might say that you stopped asking questions like that a long time ago. Have you? When you become more aware of the questions you ask, you'll be amazed at what you'll learn about yourself.

Some of the ways we allow these "please say no" questions to slip into our vocabulary are when we start questions with "I may be wrong, but. . . ." This tells the listener that we are unsure enough of our question that we can easily accept a "No." "Did you not say . . ." is another "please say no" format, because the listener has the chance to use a positive word, "Yes," which in a negatively worded question actually means no. "How can you turn this down?" is another way to ask for "No," since the question acknowledges the turn-down and demands that the listeners defend their position.

The first rule in asking questions is:

Basic Questioning Techniques

The Forced Choice Question, which in its most common forms are heard as, "Would you like this in red or blue?" or, "Will this be cash or charge?" As its name implies, the Forced Choice Question helps a customer make a decision by offering two easy selections. No matter what answer the customer chooses to give, we get the information we want and the results we desire.

A more subtle way of using this technique is to say, "When we are installing your new computer system, we can put the main cabinet in a closet or out on the production floor. The only difference is ease of accessibility for people who will be making a lot of programming changes. Which do you think would be better for Acme Widgets?" I call the phrasing around the question a drape, which softens the impact of the question. The words, "do you think" are critical, because they ask for the simple opinion of a buyer who may be afraid to make a decision.

The Multiple Choice Question is similar to the Forced Choice question, however it offers more alternatives. It is used when the buyer is capable of making a decision and is ready to buy, but responds poorly to being pressured for an order. An example would be, "These are two dollars each, ten dollars a half-dozen and thirty-five dollars for twenty-five, a tremendous savings. How many would you like?"

Closed-Ended Questions are real decision makers, but they're tough. They solicit no information, they require a commitment, and they leave little room for negotiation because they are phrased as take-it-or-leave-it questions. They can usually be answered with a yes or a no: "Do we have a deal?"

The Open-Ended Question is the obvious counterpart to the Closed-ended Question. Open-Ended Questions solicit information that will lead to the results we want. They cannot be answered with a single word and they require that the person being asked formulate an idea or a complete thought. We used Open-Ended Questions when we want information and Closed-Ended Questions when we want answers. An example of an Open-Ended Question is, "What would it take for us to make a deal today?"

Sharp Angle Questions are rarely used by professionals except in extreme situations. However, they are the most frequent types of questions used by parents, which is unfortunate because they put unnecessary strain on a relationship. Sharp Angle Questions should be used as a last resort. Typically they begin with "why" and include the word "you." For example, "Why did you do that?" and, "Why do you think delaying this purchase is in the best interest of your organization?" As you move through this book you will identify stronger, more effective questioning formats to obtain the information and results that you want.

Inverted Questions. Many years ago there was a quiz show on television called, "What's My Line?" A panel of celebrities would ask questions and try to guess an individual's occupation. A panelist could ask only Closed-Ended Questions, those that can be answered "Yes" or "No," and could ask them only as long as the answers were "Yes."

Bennett Cerf was a regular panelist who mastered the use of the Inverted Question, the ability to phrase a question in such a way that "Yes" meant no and "No" meant yes. For instance, if someone asked, "Are you not reading a book?" your answer would be "No." To answer "Yes" is to say, "Yes, I am not reading a book." Lawyers use these types of questions to trip people who are giving testimony that is not favorable to their case.

My advice is to stay away from Inverted Questions. Even if your question is answered, you can never be certain that it was understood, or that you received the information you need.

Exercising Your Questioning Skill

Let's look at how these questioning techniques can be used effectively and ineffectively, using some examples from everyday life. In the next chapter we will discuss more advanced questioning techniques, so you'll want to be comfortable with these before moving on.

The Tardy Employee. One of your subordinates is consistently late for work and your boss has looked to you to correct the problem. The actions of your subordinate are beginning to reflect on your boss' opinion of your ability to manage. What do you do?

Using traditional management techniques, the employee would be called in, chewed out and told that any future late arrivals would result in dismissal. Using the techniques in this book, we will take a totally different approach.

First, we must decide what we need to know and what we think would be the best possible outcome. In other words, how can we ask a question in a way that will give us the information we need and the results we want?

We want a productive employee, and the information we need is why the employee comes in late. Since we need accurate information, we can rule out using Inverted or Sharp Angle Questions. Perhaps we should use Open-Ended Questions to determine why the employee was consistently late, and Forced-Choice or Multiple Choice Questions to develop an action plan that will make the employee productive again.

Remember from Chapter Two that we never ask "Why/you" questions because they put the listener on the defensive. To gather information, our Open-Ended Questions might include, "What do you think is causing you to be late for work so often?" as opposed to, "Why are you always late?" We could ask, "How does your tardiness compare to the company's expectations of you?" instead of, "Why should we pay you to work here?"

To develop an action plan, try Multiple Choice Questions. "How do you think we should proceed? Should we dock your pay, suspend you for a few days, begin the termination process, or find a way for you to show the people around here how really good you are?" A Forced Choice approach would be, "Which way do I need to proceed here? Will I once again have one of the best employees in the organization, or do I need to consider replacing you?" Notice that the emphasis in the Forced Choice approach seems to be on what the manager has to do, not what the employee has to do. By taking the focus off the employee, the threat is eased and both people can become more objective.

The Tardy Teenager. Your teenage children come home an hour later than planned, and they haven't called. If we follow natural parental instincts we might tell them they're grounded for the rest of their lives. If we're using one of our questioning techniques, we would determine what we need to know and what results we want.

We need to know why our children are late, and we want them to understand what happens when they don't call. Again, stay away from the "Why/you" question. Try something like, "What happened that caused you to be late?" Then use an Open-Ended Question like, "What do you think goes on around here when you are unexpectedly late?" As they verbalize a description of their worried parents, keep saying, "That's right, and what else?" Teenagers are smart enough to figure out what's going on, and by forcing them to do more than just listen, by causing them to think, the message takes on a whole new meaning. Then we can use Multiple Choice Questions to select a form of punishment.

The Detractor. Suppose you work with a community service, volunteer or church group, where no one is paid to do anything but a lot of things need to get done. Inevitably you will encounter the Detractor. You know this individual, the one who insists that nothing is ever being done right, the one who is the first to complain and the last to help. Detractors seem more interested in keeping things from happening than in making them happen.

Usually we just try to humor Detractors as much as possible. After awhile, they may get under our skin, we might have some kind of confrontation, and things can go quickly from bad to worse. After all, Detractors have been Detractors longer than we've been producers, so they have the advantage of experience on their side. However, I'd be willing to lay odds that one can have a very successful interaction with a Detractor through the use of questioning techniques.

What we want is to make the Detractor a productive member of the organization. To accomplish that we need to know what motivates the Detractor. Here's a scenario as it might occur *without* using questions when the Detractor approaches your committee:

> DETRACTOR: "This project is all wrong. We should be helping people right here in our community, instead of doing all this stuff for people overseas."
>
> COMMITTEE MEMBER: "Blow it out your ear!"

Here's the same confrontation using the Sharp Angle Question:

> DETRACTOR: "This project is all wrong. We should be helping people right here in our community, instead of doing all this stuff for people overseas."
>
> COMMITTEE MEMBER: "Why don't you blow it out your ear!"

Now we can get serious, and deal with the Detractor using appropriate questioning techniques. Because we would be working from a defensive position, it might be best to let the Detractor develop some Multiple Choice Questions. Then, when a Multiple Choice Question is selected, it's one of several that the Detractor has created. Here's how the Forced Choice and user-defined Multiple Choice Questions would work in this situation:

> DETRACTOR: "This project is all wrong. We should be helping people right here in our community, instead of doing all this stuff for people overseas."

> COMMITTEE MEMBER: "Actually, you have a point there, Detractor." (Acknowledge the person and the idea.) "What do you think is the purpose of this organization?" (Give the Detractor a chance to vent feelings; it will happen anyway, and now you can begin to defuse them.)

> DETRACTOR: "Well, we're supposed to be a community organization that helps its own. We can't save the whole world, and there's a lot of things to be done right here in town. The homeless, or the neighborhood of elderly people in houses that need fixing up, and yet we're working on a project to help people we don't even know and who don't know us." (Detractors rarely use questions.)

> COMMITTEE MEMBER: "You know, we have a lot of talented people in our group, like you, Detractor. How should we go about deciding what projects we should undertake? Do you think a committee should do it or should we appoint one person to do it?" (Forced Choice)

> DETRACTOR: "I'd say a committee should come up with the ideas and let everybody vote on it."

Of course, this is exactly how the foreign project was chosen. To make the point, the committee member could use a Sharp Angle Question and go for the close, and the throat. That would probably embarrass and temporarily silence the Detractor, but it wouldn't create an efficient

member of the team. Whether we point it out or not, the
Detractor will realize the blunder in a matter of seconds,
so why state the obvious? Won't we just embarrass and
antagonize the Detractor further? No, we want the Detractor to be a member of our team, and we want appreciation for skipping the Detractor's little *faux pas.* To
continue:

> COMMITTEE MEMBER: "You mentioned
> some worthwhile and important projects, De-
> tractor. What would be involved in, let's say,
> fixing up those houses?"

After the Detractor rattles off what needs to be done,
ask another question:

> COMMITTEE MEMBER: "What are some dif-
> ferent ways we might get involved in that?"
> ("Ways," plural; make a multiple choice for us,
> Detractor.) "Hmmmm. Which way do you think
> would be best?"

The close could be a very subtle version of the Forced
Choice Question:

> COMMITTEE MEMBER: "What help would
> you need in order to present your ideas at one
> of the next two upcoming committee meetings?"

By questioning appropriately we have learned what we
needed to know and accomplished what we wanted. We
have asked for the Detractor's action by a specific date,
and we have involved the Detractor as a functioning
member of the group.

Irate Customers. Using questions with irate customers, instead of challenging or being defensive, can turn
those encounters into positive experiences.

Dissatisfied customers have a strong need to be heard.
They want to make sure that we know just how badly
they've been mistreated. We must allow them to vent their
hostilities before any resolution will be acceptable, and
questions are the best way to do that. The same principle applies when we are dealing with hostile members

of our family, or with angry friends. It also works in reverse. When we are the dissatisfied customer we can get the resolution we want by asking for it rather than by demanding it.

Emphasis and Inflection Can Be Everything

Once we identify what we want and we know what information we need to attain it, we can begin asking questions. However, this is where some questioners begin to falter. Just as there are better questions to ask in certain circumstances, there are also better ways of asking.

For example, read the following question five times, emphasizing the accented word each time, to see how the meaning changes.

1. *Why* are you doing that?
2. Why *are* you doing that?
3. Why are *you* doing that?
4. Why are you *doing* that?
5. Why are you doing *that*?

The first question puts listeners on the defensive and makes them feel they must justify their actions. The second challenges whether the action should be taken at all. The third asks whether the right person is doing the job. The fourth questions the method, and the fifth implies there is something else that needs to be done. The same five words, arranged in the same order, give five different messages.

The emphasis and inflection used in asking the question can determine if and how the question is answered. With the emphasis in one area and the inflection in another, the listener can give an accurate answer to the wrong question, resulting in a misunderstanding. For instance, using the five questions above, if someone wanted an answer to question #1 but used the emphasis and inflection of question #5, the listener could answer the question correctly according to what was heard, and still not provide the information needed.

This is not an uncommon occurrence. Miscommunication is the result of one of two things: either we think we understood, or we think we *were* understood. The resulting miscommunication can be humorous, or it can be disastrous.

A little girl asked her mother where she came from and the mother figured it was time for an explanation of the birds and the bees. After considerable discussion, the mother asked if she had answered the child's question. "Not exactly," said the little girl, "my friend said she came from Omaha and I just wanted to know where I came from."

Not all miscommunication is so benign. A rising executive was traveling with the big boss, trying to make a good impression. He thought it had gone well and, as the day drew to a close, the boss said, I think I'm ready for dinner, uh, do you have the time?" The young man said, Yes, sir! I just need to make a quick call." He ran to the telephone, called his wife and told her that he would be having dinner with the boss. Meanwhile the boss, whose watch had stopped running, was wondering why the young man had run off without telling him what time it was.

Make sure the question you ask is the one you want answered. How do you do that? Ask what you have asked. Before the other person has a chance to answer, follow your question with another question: "Did I make my question clear?" or, "Do you know what I'm trying to ask?" Phrasing a question like this, "Do you understand?" can make the other person defensive. Always take responsibility for making the communication clear, and phrase your questions accordingly. By asking for a restatement or reaffirmation, we can usually eliminate receiving the answer to a question we didn't mean to ask.

As a practical exercise, see how many opportunities you can find today and tomorrow to phrase things in the form of a question. This will help you develop the habit of asking, and it will help you improve as a questioner.

Claude was celebrating his first six months in New York by having Bruce and Amy to his apartment for dinner. The six months had gone by quickly because Claude had been working as many as sixty hours a week at the T-shirt shop, and then working on his apartment at night and on weekends. The building inspector, Shel, had been coming by at least once a week to see how the work was progressing, but Claude suspected that Shel was actually more interested in his landlady than in his handiwork.

The apartment was looking a lot like home to Claude. On his two trips back to Clarkesville he had picked up a couple of boxes of pictures and other accessories that helped him overcome the homesickness that occasionally hit him. Shel had helped him locate fixtures and supplies at reduced rates and, all in all, the apartment was looking sharp. It was still spartan, not at all fancy, but sharp enough for Claude.

"I have to hand it to you, Claude, I didn't think you'd make it," Bruce said. Claude was clearing away the last of the dishes from the table as Bruce and Amy sipped their coffee.

"To be honest, Cuz, there were times when I didn't think I'd make it either. But you were my inspiration, you and Larry Smith back in Clarkesville. I just couldn't let you down."

"Larry Smith . . . the insurance agent?"

"Yeah. He gave me this book. Anyway, the two of you have helped me a lot and I'll never forget it."

Amy asked, "So, how are things at the, uh, what's the name of that place where you work?" For the first time it seemed that Amy was actually showing an interest in Claude's life.

"It's called NY/NY. Actually, it's going pretty well. Bill, the owner, seems to like my work. The girl who works there, Angela, actually doesn't do much work, but she's OK."

Bruce drained the last of his coffee. "You said you've been working a lot of hours lately. Why is that?"

"Well, when Bill found out I could work with my hands he decided to rearrange the store. We're putting in some new shelves, doing a little painting, things like that. He sure is smart! I'll ask him why we're putting certain sweatshirts up front and why we're putting something else in the back and he always has a reason. He calls it 'merchandising,' but after he explains it, it just sounds like common sense." Claude was settling back in his chair now and noticed that Amy was staring at him.

"You talk better than you did a few months ago," Amy said.

"Yeah, I've been working on it."

"The southern accent is still there, but your grammar and pronunciation have really improved." Claude appreciated this unexpected attention from Amy.

"I read in this book that Larry gave me something that made me think. It said, 'The better a man speaks, the better he is understood. The better he is understood, the easier it is for success to hear him.' Pretty good, huh?"

Bruce gave a half-interested nod, but Amy was looking around the room oblivious to what Claude had said. Then she spoke. "Claude, would you like some help decorating your apartment?"

"Oh, I don't know. Christmas is not for another ten months. We can talk about it later. Besides, I'll probably just do a tree like I did last year."

"No, I mean *decorate*, you know, colors, curtains, furniture, things like that."

"Thanks, but my budget is still a little tight."

"This could be a real showplace." Amy's mind was in gear and it showed.

"We've got to go," Bruce was up and holding Amy's coat, "before that twinkle in your eye winds up breaking Claude's bank account."

The next morning Claude, following his usual routine, was at the store before anyone else. Around eight thirty, Angela called to say that she was not coming in, she thought she had the flu. Claude called Bill at home and explained the situation.

"Look," Bill said, "I have to be downtown this morning. You know how to operate the cash register, just handle it until I get there."

"But I don't know anything about sales." Claude was afraid of hurting Bill's business.

"Just be yourself, you'll do fine."

Claude had left early the night before so he'd be home in time to prepare dinner. The store needed straightening up and he was busy doing that when the first customer of the day appeared. A man in his fifties was walking around looking at various items. Claude asked, "May I help you?"

"No thanks, just looking."

"They always say that," thought Claude.

The man was walking toward a shelf that was unkempt, so Claude went over to help sort things out.

"I apologize for this mess, these are very popular shirts," Claude said.

The man stared at him for a minute and then said, "You're from the south, aren't you?"

"Yeah. Are you?"

"No, but I know people from there and they talk a lot like you."

"Oh. Where are you from?"

"I'm living in Minneapolis now, but I've lived in many places during my career."

"What do you do?"

"I'm an auditor, I conduct internal audits." Claude had no idea what the man was talking about.

"So, what brings you to New York?" Claude was still straightening the merchandise and the man was still looking at different shirts.

"I'm here for a conference. Just thought I'd take something back to our granddaughter who's staying a few days with us."

"How old is she?"

"Well, she's four. Our son and his wife are off on a trip he won for being a top salesperson in his company, so we're keeping the little girl."

"So, did you want a T-shirt or a sweatshirt?"

"Actually, I don't know what I want. I just stepped in

here out of curiosity." By now Claude and the man were chatting like they'd known each other for years.

Claude said, "I've never been to Minneapolis. It's cold there, isn't it?"

"Like you wouldn't believe!"

"Sounds like sweatshirt weather, doesn't it?"

"Guess so. What did you have in mind?"

"Look at this." Claude was holding up a pink sweatshirt with different colored balloons on it. "It's good for a giant hug. I know. I gave my little niece one for Christmas."

"Well, it is kind of cute. . . ."

"Want to score some more points? Give her mom one just like it. Your granddaughter will feel grown up and your daughter-in-law will feel special. You can't miss." Claude had found an adult size of the same shirt.

"OK, sounds good."

"What's your boy into?"

"My son? Oh, he's a golfer, fishes a little. His work keeps him so busy, though, he hardly has time for anything else."

"You're proud of him, aren't you?"

"Yes."

"It shows. Want him to think about you once a week?"

"What?"

"These sweat suits are real popular with guys your son's age. He'll wear it on weekends, around the house, to the store, things like that. You're both so busy that you may not have a chance to talk, but he'll think about you every time he puts it on. We even have a Minnesota Vikings emblem on one."

The man was holding the sweat suit and rubbing the material between his fingers. Claude turned the label inside out and said, "I noticed this when I was unpacking them. Look: made in America and machine washable. It just doesn't get any better than that, does it?"

"Looks like it would be warm and comfortable. Yes, I think he'll like that." The man was beginning to smile. "I might even enjoy wearing one myself."

"Sure you would, wouldn't you?" Claude thought he

was giving a reason why the man would make his decision. He didn't realize he was actually asking for another sale.

"OK, give me a large for my son and an extra large for me, and let me out of here before I go broke!" The man was laughing.

Claude carried the merchandise up to the cash register and began removing the price tags. "You already have something for your wife, right?"

"Yes. I found a pin in a jewelry store near the hotel." The man was nodding slightly as he spoke.

"It must be pretty. She'll love it." Claude finished stuffing the shirts and sweats into two bags when he noticed the man frowning. "Is something wrong?"

"Well, I don't think this will fit in my suitcase. I'm flying home—how will I get it there?"

Claude thought for a moment. "We could ship it, but that would take too long. Wait a minute, I'll be right back."

While he was gone two professional-looking women in their mid-thirties came into the store and began to browse. In a few seconds Claude returned from the storeroom with an Adidas athletic bag. He stuffed the two parcels of clothing into the bag, zipped it up and smiled. "There you go, all set."

"What do I owe you for the bag?"

"Actually, this guy came by last week from Adidas showing his line of clothes and gave us a couple of these. They do that, you know. Just take it and thanks for your business."

The men shook hands and the customer left. Claude turned his attention to the two women who were browsing. Before he could say a word, one of them spoke up. "Do we get a free bag, too?"

"Ma'am?" Claude stammered.

"Well, that man got a free bag, do we?" The women looked at each other and winked.

"Oh. He needed a way to get his stuff home and I had this bag, so I gave it to him." Claude was earnestly trying to explain his actions.

"We're just teasing. Where are you from?"

"Clarkesville, Georgia. Where are you from?"

"Well, I live here in the city and my friend is from Boston. She's just visiting me for a few days to get some *decent* food and to see some *real* theater." They looked very professional but they were giggling like schoolgirls.

Claude thought for a moment. "What shows did you see?"

"Well, we saw 'Phantom' Friday night, and 'Cats' for the third time on Saturday."

"Wow," Claude said, "I was here three months before I saw even one show. Which one did you like best?"

"Of course 'Cats' is always great, but I really like 'Phantom,'" the one from Boston said. "Not many of my friends have seen it, but they've all seen 'Cats.'"

"Would you like a 'Phantom' sweatshirt? It would remind your friends that you've seen the show, and it would remind you how great it was. We've got them in pink and black and white, I think. No, we're out of the black ones, they're the most popular." Claude was looking through the shelves as he talked.

The woman from New York put a false pout on her face and said, "Aw, we wanted a black one!"

"Well, I'm sorry but we're out of them. Did you both want one?"

"Yes, and one for our friends in Boston, too." The two women were elbowing each other and having a difficult time keeping a straight face. They were having fun playing with the country bumpkin.

"Wouldn't a white one look just as nice?" Claude was trying to please his customers so they would not leave disappointed. Then it hit him. He looked at the two women, smiled and said, "How many friends do you have in Boston?"

"Six, and all of them wanted a 'Phantom' shirt."

"Stay right where you are," Claude shouted. He had just remembered something.

Another trip to the back room, a quick dig through the unopened boxes and Claude had his treasure. He walked out of the storeroom with eight black 'Phantom' sweatshirts. Instead of being grateful, the two women looked like they were about to faint.

"Will eight be enough?" Claude asked.

"More than enough," one of them groaned.

"I picked up your free Adidas bag, too. Will that be cash or charge?"

The two women were smiling, but not as talkative, when they left. That's when Claude noticed Bill standing by the door.

"That was pretty good, Claude. I didn't know you could sell." Bill was reaching out to shake Claude's hand. "The way you handled those two was great!"

Claude was confused. "I didn't know I was selling. Besides I was only trying to find them what they wanted."

"Right. And what's all this about a free bag?"

Claude explained about the earlier customer and the problem he was facing getting his merchandise home. As he talked, Bill went over to the cash register. When Claude had finished his story, Bill said, "These two sales total more than five hundred dollars. Our average sale is usually under fifty dollars. How did you do that?"

"Well, I'm not really sure. I just asked the man about his family and what he did for a living, and I asked the women what shows they had seen ..."

Bill interrupted him, "Well, whatever it is keep it up. You're now our new salesman."

Claude thought for a minute and then asked, "Does that mean I get a raise?"

Bill was caught off guard. "I'll tell you what. I'll pay you a commission, how would that be?"

Claude had been paid a commission when he worked at the lumber yard, and the extra money had been great. "How much will my commission be, Bill?"

Bill took out a piece of scrap paper and began writing some numbers on it. As he did, a customer walked in and Claude, the new salesman, went over to help. The customer was a man in his thirties wearing a Brooks Brothers suit, wing tip shoes and a Rolex watch. He walked over to the section marked "Children's Sizes."

Claude studied the man for a moment and asked, "You're looking for something for your niece, right?"

"How did you know?"

"I don't know," Claude said, "you just sorta' have that uncle look about you."

"It's her birthday and I'll be home next weekend, so I thought I'd take her a shirt or something."

"How old is she?"

"Three, well, she'll be four by the time I get home." By now the customer was thumbing through some sweatshirts.

"Where's home for you?" Claude asked, almost ignoring the previous response.

"A little town outside of Pittsburgh," the man said, "called McKeesport. Ever been there?"

"Nope. Does it get real cold there?"

"About like New York," the man said. "You're not from here, are you? You sound like my cousins from Alabama."

"Actually, I'm from Georgia. What does your niece like to do? What's she into?"

"I don't know. What does a three-year-old do?"

"I wouldn't know either, except my niece, who's about the same age, keeps me informed. Has your niece, uh, what's her name?"

"Heather," he answered.

"Has Heather ever mentioned Sesame Street, Big Bird, Cookie Monster, or anything like that?" Claude was walking toward some brightly colored shirts at the end of one of the displays.

"As a matter of fact she has." The customer was smiling and following Claude.

"Here's a bunch of different shirts with Sesame Street characters in New York. You can tell Heather that you live close to where Bert and Ernie live. You can bring her this one. It shows Kermit and Miss Piggy in Central Park. Here's one with Miss Piggy at Tavern On the Green. Heather Probably likes pink, right?

"Uh, I guess so. Which one do you think I should get her?"

"Well, you know her, but you can't miss with the Kermit and Miss Piggy one." Claude was holding up the shirt.

"I kind of prefer the pink Miss Piggy at the restaurant. I wonder which one Heather would like."

In all innocence Claude answered, "They're only $24.99, get 'em both. Get two hugs instead of one."

The man thought for a minute and smiled. "You're right. Why not?"

As Claude rang up the sale the man began looking through the smaller items on display at the counter. He held up a pen and asked, "Is this indelible?"

"It won't wash out if that's what you want to know. Why do you ask?" Claude was curious.

"I just had an idea. Maybe I could put Heather's name on the shirts, or something."

Claude's face lit up. "I know! Put Miss Piggy's signature on it. Have her say, 'Happy Birthday, Heather,' or something."

"That's a great idea. Let's see, I could get one of the people in my office with a real nice handwriting to do the actual writing. I'll just have to think of something clever to say. Put this pen in there with the shirts."

After the man left, Claude went back to where Bill was standing to continue their conversation. Bill held up the piece of paper he had been working on and said, "How does this sound, Claude? We keep your pay at the same level and then you make a commission of five percent on everything you sell. What do you think?"

"Well, I guess it sounds OK. You've got yourself a new salesperson, Bill."

The next day Bill gave Angela the choice of being responsible for stocking the shelves or quitting, and Angela quit. Until Bill could hire a replacement stock boy, Bill and Claude came in earlier than usual, and stayed later, to keep the shelves stocked and the store clean.

Later that same week, three women came in during the lunch hour and walked over toward the children's clothing. Claude watched them for a moment, went over and asked, "You're having a shower, right?"

One of the women looked at him and asked, "Why do you say that?"

"Well," Claude said, "y'all came in together, went right for the children's things and that's how women generally do when they shop for a baby shower present. How close was I?"

"Close. Actually, our coworker came back from lunch the other day with an autographed Miss Piggy sweatshirt. It was so cute we decided to buy some for people we know." The taller woman was talking to Claude as the others held up various shirts.

"Great idea," said Claude. "You know that he actually bought a pen and autographed them himself, don't you?"

"Yes. It's a terrific idea. The child's name on the shirt looks personalized . . ., " the taller lady was becoming engrossed in the shirts.

At the checkout counter, Claude showed the women the various pen colors and each customer chose a different one. He rang up their order, thanked them for their business and watched a man come into the store as the women went out.

This was a man who would change Claude's life.

CHAPTER FOUR

Advanced Questioning Techniques

This chapter will offer some advanced questioning techniques that everyone can use. If you think you shouldn't try the advanced techniques because you've never used those described in Chapter Three, think again. Wouldn't it be great if you could begin asking for things in an advanced manner? What would it mean to you if you could use these techniques effortlessly and cause people to give you information they have not shared before?

Listening Is An Art Form

One of the main elements of a successful transaction is the ability to listen. Everyone keeps as a secret the one thing it would take for them to do business with you today. If we don't ask, nine times out of ten they won't tell us; if we do ask, nine times out of ten they will. We have to ask, and then listen.

When I close a sale I know that the customer has to voice objections. If I try to deny that opportunity, closing the sale becomes very difficult. Customers need to say, "Your price is too high," "I need to think about it," "Your competition looks better," before they can justify buying in their own mind.

It's an essential part of the process, like warm-ups for a runner. A smart runner knows that it's important to stretch their key muscles prior to running a marathon.

No serious person would consider denying an athlete that opportunity. By allowing the listener to vent their superficial answers, you have made it easier for them to be thoughtful and to and offer a meaningful response.

People need the opportunity to vent their feelings. One of the things we teach salespeople is, "When customers feel they need to talk, they deserve to be heard." In other words, let them talk. Everyone wants to feel that their message has been delivered and received. Most customer service complaints can be resolved just by letting customers state their case and ask for the resolution they want. What they want is usually something we would consider reasonable anyway. Unreasonable demands typically come from customers who feel they have been slighted in the past and now want something extra to make up for what they perceive to be past deficiencies.

The Three-Question Technique

TIP #7

Ask the same question three times, three different ways and take the third answer. You'll be very close to the truth.

In the previous chapter we saw a common scenario as two people passed in the hall, the "How are you, Fine/How are you" non-event. Have you ever wondered how that works? By observing others you will come to understand that the first answer most people give to a question is the one they think the other person wants to hear. When we ask people how they are, they will say, "Fine," whether they are fine or not. They are giving us the answer they think we want to hear. In fact, people are rarely ever fine. "Fine" is that thin line that distinguishes between "things are going great" and "things aren't going so well." We use fine because it is what we think the other person wants to hear. If you don't believe this, try answering the next, "How are you?" with how you really feel, and see if anybody cares.

So how do you get a straight answer? Ask the same question three times, three different ways and take the third answer. Here's an example. We want to know from our customer how well our company is doing as compared to our competitors. The information will help us to serve our customers better, and to increase our revenues and profits. So we call up one of our customers and ask, "How are we doing?" What is the customer most likely to say? "Fine!" Now there's some information we can use! That's exactly what we needed to know in order to serve our customers better, right? It is, in fact, useless information.

Why did we get that answer? The customer thought it was what we wanted to hear, and it was a fast way to chase us out of the customer's busy day. However, we still need the information, so we rephrase the question and ask again: "How could we serve you better?" The second question usually brings up an unrealistic expectation. The customer could respond with a variation on the following theme: "Well, you could cut your price, shorten your delivery time, gold plate your product and give better customer service." If we could do those things we would have done them a long time ago. Not only are these unrealistic expectations, but the customer knows it. Now what?

We ask the same question, rephrased, a third time. "You're a smart business person," we would say to the customer, "if you ran our company, what would you do differently?" Now we should start taking notes; after the third iteration of the same question, the customer really opens up.

A little analysis explains this phenomenon. Because of the ways we have programmed ourselves, we must allow the old messages to be deleted before we can create new ones. What we want from the customer in this case is a fresh answer to an old question. By asking three times we allow customers to "use up" the obvious answers and give them time to realize we're after something with substance. Thus, we cause them to think and to come up with some answers that have greater depth and therefore greater value.

As a manager who wants to be more effective, try asking your subordinates, "How am I doing?" How are they most likely to answer? "Fine." Why? Because they think that's what you want to hear and, besides, their raise or promotion depends on your liking them. So, rephrase the question and ask, "How could I be a better manager?" Here comes the unrealistic expectation. "Well, you could give us longer lunch breaks, let us leave early on Fridays and you could have my office redecorated." All of these are unrealistic expectations. Ask a third time after all of the superficial and obvious answers have been given. "If you were managing this department with our current objectives, what would you do differently?" The third answer will contain some information you can use.

By the time you get to the third question, your customers understand you are asking as one businessperson to another. You are requesting that they factually and realistically consider what changes they would make in your company. The longer they pause before answering this one, the better the answer will be. Whatever the answer is, listen closely. They are telling you what it would take to get more business from them.

For instance, if they say, "I would have my salespeople spend more time with the customers," they are really saying, "You need to spend more time with me." If they say, "I would change the product mix," they are really saying, "Your product line needs to be overhauled to suit my needs." When they say something like, "I would have them focus on what the competition is doing," they are really saying, "I like you, but your competition is about to convince me that they have the upper hand in the following areas. . . ."

Listen closely to the third response, no matter what it is. Even if it sounds superficial there is probably a grain of truth in it somewhere. When a customer offers a third response like, "Well, shoot, I'd throw a party for all of our great customers . . . like ME," it sounds facetious but this client is using the opportunity to tell you that some wining and dining might be in order.

To use the three-question technique effectively, it helps if we think about the questions in advance to anticipate how we will word them. Since responses to the first question are usually predictable, we have a good idea how to phrase the second question. How well we know the person with whom we're speaking may help us to know what direction the second response will take. Therefore, formulating the third question should focus on what we really need to know, and what information this person has that will help you reach your objective.

Here are some examples. Suppose you're talking to that employee who's consistently late for work, the one we met in Chapter Three. You already know that the first response to your bringing up the tardiness problem will be what caused the lateness today. What you really want your subordinates to realize is that a routine has been established, a behavior pattern that is making them late for work frequently. Using the three-question technique, the conversation might go something like this:

> YOU: "What makes you late for work so often?" (The employee will hear, "What MADE you late for work today?")
>
> EMPLOYEE: "There was a lot of traffic on the freeway."
>
> YOU: "Don't you allow for traffic tie-ups when you plan your morning?"
>
> EMPLOYEE: "Well, it isn't usually this bad."
>
> YOU: "What changes will you make in your morning routine to ensure that you arrive at work on time every day?"

If you try to put the third question first, the employee would simply blame the immediate circumstances:

> YOU: "What changes will you make in your morning routine to ensure that you arrive at work on time every day?"

EMPLOYEE: "Well, today there was a traffic jam on the freeway. . . ."

The owner of a major property management company has a monthly meeting with each of her supervisors, the people responsible for keeping the apartments rented and well maintained. She evaluates the performance of each supervisor in several categories, such as how many people came by to see the property, how many actually rented a unit, how many current tenants extended their leases, etc. The owner knows that whenever there's a problem in one of these areas the supervisor inevitably wants to explain (offer an excuse for) the poor performance. All the owner wants to know was, "What do you plan to do about it?" She does not want to hear the excuses. If she asked, "What do you plan to do about this problem?" she might hear, "The weather was terrible last month." Therefore, she learned to ask questions that she did not even want answered or that she already knew the answer to, in order to control the monthly interview. Her meeting now goes something like this:

Question #1: "What happened last month that kept your number of visits so low?"

Actually, she really doesn't care; last month is gone.

Question #2: "How many visits would we need this month to make up for last month?"

She already knows; she can add and subtract.

Question #3: "What will you do about it?"

The three-question technique gives the property supervisors the opportunity to vent their feelings before addressing the issue, and allows the owner to avoid the frustration she would feel if she did not know this was a three-step process.

Try the three question technique as an exercise on this imaginary irate customer. Standing in front of you is a customer, holding one of your products, talking loudly and very red in the face. He tells you that this product has been in for repair three times and it still doesn't work.

What does the customer want? What three questions do you ask?

The customer wants someone to acknowledge that he's been mistreated, that his is a legitimate complaint, and that he will not be saddled with a defective product or a lifetime of service calls. When we don't receive the service we believe we're entitled to, we take it personally. When others seem to be receiving better service, we take it personally. This customer still wants to do business with you or he would have written you off a couple of repairs ago, but he also wants to be respected.

Using the three-question technique, here is how you can apologize, show respect and satisfy the irate customer:

> YOU: "We've done a terrible job of taking care of great customer, haven't we?" (Accept responsibility)

> CUSTOMER: "You sure have!" (Confirmation)

> YOU: "I apologize, Mr. Customer, this is really not like us, is it?" (This makes it easy for him to continue doing business with you without losing face)

> CUSTOMER: "No, you guys are usually better that this." (Confirmation)

> YOU: "What do I" (not "we") "need to do to make this right?"

Asking the last question first could bring a very different answer. The customer might begin by demanding an apology, an explanation, perhaps a meeting with the president. Why? Because even though you may have *said* it, he could not *hear* as the first question, "What do I need to do to make this right?" His anger was not yet defused, so all he could hear was, "So, what do you expect me to do about it?" By going through the process of this technique, he had a chance to vent his feelings, to be acknowledged, and to get an accurate understanding of your sincere response.

By thinking through what the other person wants, what

you want to accomplish and what the best result could ultimately be, you will be able to formulate the questioning pattern. The more you use this technique, the easier it becomes.

Built-In Assumptions

If you're a get-it-done, cut-to-the-chase kind of person and you want to eliminate the three question exercise, try this technique:

TIP #8

Build an assumption into the question in such a way that, no matter how they answer, they are verifying the assumption

---

Lawyers use this one a lot. The classic example is, "Are you still beating your wife?" Any attempt to answer the question verifies the assumption. By being more subtle than that, we can use the assumption technique to garner other information. The important point to remember is that we don't care what the answer is, all that matters is that the person tries to answer the question.

You are a sales manager, one of your best salespeople has just returned from a call that went badly, and you want to know what happened. The salesperson is a seasoned professional and you don't see the need to play the three-question game. Ask a question like, "When did you realize you were losing control of the interview?" The assumption is that the salesperson lost control of the call at some point, and a good salesperson would be able, in retrospect, to see when it happened. By answering the question and telling you where the critical error was made, the salesperson is acknowledging that the customer was allowed to take control of the call.

As you have learned, it is dangerous to ask a "why" question because people immediately become defensive when they hear one. But using an assumptive "why" question can bring some interesting results. "Why did you feel it was necessary to insult the customer while filling out the form?" is an example. Answering the question acknowledges that the salesperson insulted the customer.

Salespeople use many assumptive questions because they are effective. One that I like is, "Besides the price, Ms. Customer, what other objections would you have to buying this today?" The assumption is that price will be an objection, and I just need to know what other objections there may be. Unless the customer says something like, "No, no, the price is OK, it's the color I don't like," I know I need to sell the value of the product. She has verified the assumption that price is an issue even if she lists 1,000 other reasons for not buying.

"Are you going to the party with Bob?" is the parents' way of finding out if a child is going to a party they've heard rumors about. "Will the people in our Minnesota plant be affected by the layoffs?" is a subordinate's way of finding out if the boss knows anything about some upcoming personnel actions.

I once worked in an office with a very effective grapevine, except when it came to promotions. The manager of that facility had a way of keeping all promotions under wraps until he was ready to announce them. Larry was up for a promotion to our headquarters in New Jersey but no one knew if it had come through, and it was driving us crazy. If he had been promoted, at least two people would know: Larry and the manager. The manager was too shrewd for me, so I walked up to Larry when no one else was around and asked, "Did the price of New Jersey real estate scare you?" His answer was, "At first it did but the company's relocation plan helps a lot, you know." In this case the real assumption, "Did you get the promotion," was hidden in another assumption: the promotion required a move. Larry would not know the details of the move until he had been offered the job.

Of course, part of building an assumption into a question is a matter of bluffing. You have to make the other person believe that you know something that, indeed, you may not know. In 1922, the secretary of the interior, Albert Fall, had abused the authority that President

Harding had given him, an abuse that would later be known as the Teapot Dome Scandal. A press conference was called for two o'clock in the afternoon but most reporters were in the White House before lunch just to see what the other reporters knew. Everyone wanted a "scoop" but no one knew why the press conference was being held. One respected reporter walked into a presidential aide's office, sat down, lit a cigar, chatted for a while and then said, "It's a damn shame Fall has to resign, isn't it?" "Yeah, the President really likes him," replied the aide. A few minutes later the reporter left and did not attend the press briefing. The reporters who did attend learned that Fall was resigning. When they left around two thirty, they found paper boys already hawking copies of a certain newspaper carrying the headline, "FALL RESIGNS."

The Third Party

TIP #9

Introduce A Third Party Into Your Question

Have you ever noticed how some people respond to your question by asking for repeated clarification? They want to know how you want the question answered. They don't want to offend or appear stupid, so they hedge around the answer long enough to figure out what an appropriate response might be. You can eliminate this exercise by introducing a third party into your question. Instead of asking, "What do you think of my idea?" try asking, "What do you think Mr. Johnson will think of my idea?"

Look at how this works. Joe, the person you asked, is free to say anything he wishes because you're not asking what Joe thinks, you're asking what Mr. Johnson thinks. Mr. Johnson may never have discussed the idea, but Joe is free to talk. When you introduce a third party, the information you receive is coming from the heart and mind of the individual answering the question, not the third party. Even if Joe has discussed the idea with Mr.

Johnson, he'll still be giving his version of Johnson's opinion. Either way, it tells you more about the person answering the question than it does about the third party.

Using a third party puts you and the person being questioned figuratively on the same side of the desk. It seems as if the two of you are discussing a third entity. Try using different third parties. Ask how the person thinks your peers, subordinates and superiors would think. Ask them how the president of the company (or the United States) would think. As long as Joe feels he is speaking for someone else, he will speak less guardedly.

You might even try combining techniques. A client asked me to come look at his business, a privately-held company bearing the owner's name. His name was everywhere, on the products, on the signs and on the paychecks. Everyone knew who the boss was.

As I drove up and walked through the production facilities there was every sign of decaying morale. The grass needed cutting and paint was peeling. Inside, there was waste everywhere, employees were moving slowly and lackadaisically. There was no enthusiasm and no energy in the place.

After meeting with the owner for awhile, I learned that whenever he was having a bad day he would go out on the production floor and fire somebody. It just sort of cheered him up. As you might imagine, people were afraid of him, intimidated by him and losing respect for him. I decided to work on that assumption, his people were losing respect for him and that's why morale was low, productivity was down and waste was up.

He told me that he had called an employee meeting to find out what was wrong. He brought all 250 employees into the cafeteria and asked, "What's wrong around here?" How do you think the employees responded? They gave him a unanimous, "Everything's fine." After all, this is a man who fires people for a good time! How else could they answer? That's when he called me.

I said, "Look, I know you've asked them once, but we really need to go back and ask again. I think the problem is that your employees have lost respect for you and we need to find out why. Then we can do some things to restore their respect. Let's build that assumption into a question and see how your people respond. Go down to the production floor and pick out an employee. Anybody. Ask this question, 'Why don't you respect me?' "

He did and it didn't work.

This is a boss who enjoys firing people. Now he's going around asking employees a pointed question that, if answered truthfully, is liable to get them a pink slip. Of course they didn't respond. He came back to his office and told me he hadn't learned anything. He had gone up to an employee named Robby and said, "Robby, why don't you respect me?" Robby effectively dodged the question after stammering around for a while.

"Here's what I want you try next," I said. "Introduce a third party." We formulated a question and the client went back and found Robby.

"Robby, why doesn't William respect me?" he asked. All of a sudden Robby felt free to talk, even though Robby and William had never discussed the subject. My client got an ear full.

He came back to his office with three pages of notes. I said, "Great! Now what are you going to do with this information?" He said, "Fire William." We talked about what had happened and, of course, he didn't fire William. But he did learn an important technique that continues to serve him well.

The $75,000 Question

This technique got its name because I used it to generate $75,000 in consulting fees in one year.

Would you like it?

It's the single most powerful sales tool I have found.

Do you want it?

It is also the single most effective management tool I have found.

Would you like to know what it is?

Before I tell you, I need a commitment that you will

never use it on me. If we ever meet at a conference or in a restaurant, you cannot use this question on me. Fair enough? If you agree, here's the question:

"I DON'T KNOW, WHAT DO YOU THINK?"

Sounds like an innocent question, doesn't it? That one question has opened more doors for me and brought me more concrete information than any other question I have found. You can use it on the telephone and it will bring you powerful, useful information. Because it sounds so innocent, the question catches people off-guard, and they will tell you things they had no intention of telling you before.

TIP #10

When You Want Information, Ask For An Opinion

"I don't know, what do you think?" Dissect that question and you will see why it works. The first half of the question says, "I may not know the best answer," a statement that leaves an opening for creative solutions.

Suppose you have worked for a company for twenty years and for the past twenty years you have been handling a certain problem in a certain way. A new employee comes to work, sees the same problem for the first time, and asks you how to solve it. Most people would say, "I've seen this problem a hundred times before and every time I see it I use this solution. ..." What have you taught that individual? You have suggested that you are the great knower-of all-solutions and that the new employee should come to you whenever there's a problem.

Just because we have successfully used a certain solution 100 times does not mean we have found the best solution. It only means we have found one that works. The new person will see the problem differently and, if challenged to find a solution, may find one that you and I would never think of in a lifetime.

Each of us makes decisions based on our unique talents, skills and experiences. Everybody has a different set of each of these so we arrive at decisions differently. Asking the new person to solve the problem gives us insight into that individual's perspective, gives us a new solution that might really work, and gives us an opportunity to learn something. Even if the proposed new idea didn't work, it might open our minds to new ideas. If we aren't willing to see the problem and the solution from the perspective of others, how will we grow?

The second half of the question, "what do you think," gives the other person the license and the motivation to tell us what they think. It encourages them to open up, and makes them the authority.

Try this question and you will find it opening doors and bringing you information you never thought was available. It's so effective that I would like to tell you that I'm a genius, and that I created it all by myself. Actually, it came about as a matter of survival.

A client had called me in to do some consulting. As I walked through his outer office, I saw something that appeared to be a problem. In his office, the client began describing the symptoms of the problem I had just seen in his outer office. He had seen it so often that, although he could identify the symptoms, he could not see the problem anymore.

After we had talked for a while I said, "I need to verify some assumptions. I'll be back in a little while." I went down to the production floor and, sure enough, there was the problem. I went to the sales department and verified the problem. I went to see the numbers people and had them quantify the cost of the problem. Then I returned to the owner's office. It was not even noontime on my first day; I was breaking records for consulting.

"I'm ready to make a recommendation," I said. "No," said the client, "you need to hear the history of the company first."

Did I need to hear the history of the company? Of course not. Did he need to tell me the history of the company? YES! Remember, when the customer perceives they need to talk, the customer deserves to be heard. Besides, I charge by the hour. He can tell me the history of the Roman Empire if he wants to. So I settled back in my chair, took out pen and paper and prepared to listen.

Unfortunately, this man is a Southern Gentleman who talks very slowly and speaks in a monotone. I could physically stay in the room with him but my mind would wander off. Whenever I caught my mind in some faraway place, I would force my attention back into the room, only to have it wander again almost immediately. At one point, when my mind was about as far away as it could be, I realized that the room had suddenly become very quiet. I thought to myself, "Uh-oh, he's asked me a question, and I didn't hear it!"

I looked at him and said, "I don't know, what do you think?" and he was good for another two hours!

Jeopardy Selling. This is a technique for you advanced salespeople. I call it "Jeopardy Selling," after the popular game show on television called Jeopardy. On this program contestants are required to phrase their answers in the form of a question. In Jeopardy Selling, we phrase everything in the form of a question. There are two simple rules to follow in this sophisticated sales technique:

1. Never make a statement

2. Never answer a customer's question until you are ready to close.

I know it sounds strange, contradictory to everything you've been taught about sales. As you become more and more proficient in the use of questions, you will find it less and less necessary to make statements. In fact, you will find value and success in using questions, and you will automatically use fewer statements.

Think about this for a moment. You probably have heard the principle that in negotiations the first person to speak loses. When the offer is on the table and it is not exactly what every party wants, the first person to react is the one who will make the initial and probably the greatest concessions. Do you know why that is? An offer on the table is virtually the same thing as having a question on the table. The offer is not what either party would choose so the question becomes, "What are we going to do about it?"

The first person to speak will usually address the fact that the offer, as is, is unacceptable. Then an area of compromise will be mentioned and a concession suggested. The way to control negotiations is to keep the other person talking. The way to control a sales situation is to keep the other person talking. When the other person asks a question it is often one sentence long. To answer it properly, we will probably use many sentences. So who is controlling the conversation?

Perhaps you can remember your mother telling you that it is not polite to answer a question with a question. Now, I know better than to go against anything our mothers taught us, but the fact is that Mom's rules don't apply in this situation. It is OK to answer a question with a question. In fact, it is essential that we do, if we are to get what we want.

Here's an example. As a professional speaker I am required to have a rate card. My rate card is time sensitive, which means that for a certain amount of time I charge a certain amount of money. For a 90 minute presentation I charge $X, for a half day $Y and for a full day $Z. These rates are published and I cannot deviate from them except under specific circumstances, or I'll be in trouble with the agents and bureaus around the country who represent me.

When someone calls me and the first question they ask is what I charge for a 90 minute presentation, can I answer their question? Of course I can, but if I answer the question I will lose the speaking engagement nine out of ten times. Why? Because I have not established value in the customer's mind. Either my fee sounds too high and they become defensive and terminate the call, or my fee is too low and I couldn't possibly be a good enough speaker for their group.

So, what do I do? I ask a question, like "Tell me about your group; who will be there?" or "What do you want to accomplish at your conference?" The truth is that I may not even be the right speaker for that group. Maybe the meeting planner is looking for someone who knows a topic that I am good at addressing, but there are other speakers who are experts on the subject. As a professional, I should refer the meeting planner to a better-qualified speaker. Until I have asked questions I don't know who the customer is, I don't understand the needs, and I have not established any value in the customer's mind.

After the customer has given me an idea about the expectations of the participants, I explain what I would do to help meet those expectations. Before we hang up, I tell them my fee. It's exactly the same fee I would have quoted in the beginning of the conversation but, as a result of the questions and answers, the fee has value and relevance and my chances of closing the speaking engagement have gone up dramatically.

Remember, never answer a customer's question, never make a statement until you're ready to close.

If we answer the customer's question, we allow the customer to take control of the interaction. When we respond to our children's questions, we allow them to take control of the conversation. When we respond to our boss' question, we allow the boss to take control of the discussion. Don't we really want the ideas of the other person? Don't we really want information?

A "sale" might be getting a raise or some other concession from your superiors. Control the situation, don't answer their questions. A "sale" might be motivating your children to do something they had not planned to do, like cleaning their rooms. Control the encounter, don't answer their questions. When they ask, "Isn't it my room? Who cares if it's a little cluttered?" you could answer, "I CARE!" or, "The health department was by again this week. . . ." Instead, ask a question like, "Tell me three reasons why you enjoy having the kitchen clean," or, "It's your room, but whose house is it?"

In my seminars, people frequently ask me how I come up with these questions. When I tell them, they often say something like, "I'll never be that creative." That's an erroneous statement for two reasons. One is that, indeed, they are creative. They might not come up with exactly

the same question I did, but they could come up with a
question, one that might even be better than mine. The
second reason is that creativity has little to do with it.
The easiest way I have found to formulate questions is
to use the following technique:

Second Generation Questions are those that eliminate
the first question by assuming that it was already asked,
that it got the response you wanted, and that you are
ready to ask the next logical question.

For instance, if you want to discuss a raise with your
boss you might start by asking how well the boss thinks
you're doing. Then, you might ask the boss to consider
an increase in compensation. Using the Second Generation Question, you would assume that the boss had given
you a positive response to the first question and then start
with the second question. "Since I have met or exceeded
the objectives you and the company have given me, isn't
it about time we reviewed my compensation?"

This form of questioning gets us down to business
quickly. It eliminates falling into an established pattern
of conversation. Since established patterns are usually
used by others to get them what *they* want, we need to
avoid them.

Salespeople can use this technique effectively to close
sales. Since closing usually means asking for the order
and facing possible rejection, using the second generation question circumvents the typical closing scenario.
When the salesperson asks for the order, all of the energy in the room is focused on the decision. The buyer
feels pressure to make the "right" decision and typically
opts for more objections. The seller is nervous about the
showdown; this is high noon in Dodge City. No wonder
palms are sweaty, people stop making rational decisions

to buy and, instead, try to think of new objections. This whole scenario can be avoided by using Second Generation Questions.

Suppose you are the salesperson. You have asked the customer for the order and you got a "yes," the answer you wanted. What would your next question be? You would probably ask something like, "Would you like to have this delivered on Tuesday or Thursday?" or, "Which color did you want?" Start with one of those questions instead. It avoids the uncomfortable "closing" atmosphere, and causes the customer to focus on what they will have, not what they are spending. This is sometimes known as an assumptive close, but if you see it as Second Generation Questioning you will be able to use it more often and more effectively, and you will find opportunities to use it in non-sales situations.

After spending more than 100 nights a year on the road for the past several years I have learned that the front desk clerk at the hotel can usually affect what kind of stay I'm going to have by determining which room I will be given. When the reservations are made by my staff or my client, the hotel may or may not be able to honor my request for a king size bed, a quiet room, etc., because I usually check in late in the evening. Instead of asking, "Do you have any king rooms left?" I assume that they do and I start with the next question, "Which one of your available king rooms would you say is the quietest?" Usually they do not even stop to see if I have requested a king, before they begin looking for one.

A sense of humor helps, of course. Front desk people are usually the ones who receive the brunt of the fallout from other people's mistakes. When the travel agent fails to tell the traveler that the room isn't guaranteed, it's the front desk person who gets chewed out. When room service runs late, the front desk clerk will hear about it the next morning. What question does the front desk clerk want to hear? What can I say to that person that will show respect, give them a chuckle and, in the process, cause them to give me a nice room? Some of the questions I have used may imply that they are Second Generation Questions by having built-in assumptions. One that does well is, "Can you help insulate me from the press?" This implies that the press would be interested in reaching me, therefore I must be Somebody. Another is, "Who's using your suites tonight?" This one will find me sleeping in a suite at no additional cost in about one out of five attempts. Other questions that work are, "What color is the jacuzzi in this room?"

Once I checked into a Pickett Suites Hotel in Orlando around midnight. I had not eaten all day, and I asked the front desk clerk how late their room service ran. All the hotel's food services were closed, the nearest restaurant was miles away and I did not have a car. A few minutes after walking into my room the manager appeared with a sandwich and glass of milk. This was first class customer service in response to a traveler's question, and now I cannot say enough nice things about Pickett Suites or stay there often enough.

With practice, you will feel comfortable using second generation questions. Then you can move on to the next level.

TIP #12

Assume that you asked the second question and got the answer you wanted, what would your next question be? Start with that one!

Third Generation Questions are similar to Second Generation Questions, but Third Generation Questions assume that you got the answer you wanted to the first two questions. What would your third question be? Start with that one.

A furniture salesman had helped a couple narrow their choices for a pit group to three, to two and finally to one. It was time to close. Instead of asking for the order, instead of asking what day they wanted it delivered, he said, "Picture this pit group in your family room with your existing tables, lamps and accessories. What else do we need to add?" Using a single question he had moved past the agreement to buy, the delivery (his question assumed the furniture was in their home) on to the next step: additional sales.

Third generation questions are tougher to use because the opportunities are not as obvious. But with practice, you will become proficient with them especially as you use Second Generation Questions more frequently.

Constantly ask yourself, "If I ask this question and get the answer I want, what would my next question be?" Then put yourself in the habit of asking, "If the answers to my first two questions are what I want, what will my next question be?"

I had a neighbor named Tom who had the only ladder in the neighborhood that would reach my gutters. Tom was known to be more than a little stingy with his things. If I asked to borrow his ladder, I thought he would say no. One day I knocked on Tom's door and asked, "Are you going to clean my gutters, or what?"

I wish I had taken a camera to preserve the look on his face. Finally he composed himself enough to say, "Clean your gutters?"

"Well," I said, "the least you can do then is loan me your ladder." He did.

It is the combination of humor, assumptive use of questions and believing you know how the other person will answer that gives you the edge in asking for what you want.

Self-Evaluation Questions. We often find ourselves in the position of having to critique the work of our employees or our children. It is easy for most of us to tell them what they are doing right, it is more difficult to tell them what they are doing that needs improvement. The principle behind the Self-Evaluation technique is that people know when their performance is up to standard. When they think they have done a better job than their superior thinks, it is usually because they did not understand the performance standard.

Since people can usually judge their own performance as it compares to a known expectation, why not let them do the critique? Ask a question like, "How do you think you did?" Watch what happens: the person being asked has the opportunity to assess their own performance. It saves us having to do the entire critique. Since they will know some of the mistakes they made, they will mention them and save us the discomfort. If they miss any weaknesses we can mention them later.

My experience with this technique is that people will usually be harder on themselves than others will. By using this process you will save yourself the aggravation of being the fault-finder and you will see how well the other person understands what is expected of them.

The Story Continues . . .

The man who came into NY/NY that afternoon was, as far as Claude could tell, just like any other customer. He was looking around but not at anything in particular. Claude just watched him. Finally the man picked up a sweatshirt with the logo of the top Broadway play, "Cats."

Claude walked over to the man and asked, "Did you like the play?"

"What play?" the man asked.

"Cats." Claude was pointing to the logo on the shirt.

"Oh. Oh, yes, it was great. Have you seen it?"

Claude smiled and said, "Yep. I've seen several shows since I've been here, and 'Cats' is still my favorite. What's yours?"

"Phantom. Same producer, you know, but I just like the staging better." As he spoke the man noticed Claude had begun moving across the aisle.

"Have you seen this shirt?" Claude was holding up a shirt with the "Phantom of the Opera" logo on it.

"No, I haven't. That's kind of nice," the man said as he took the shirt.

"Is this for you or for someone else?" Claude asked.

"It's for my brother and sister-in-law. My wife and I moved here about a year ago. We'll be going out to visit my brother and I just thought it would be nice to take them something from the city. You know, something that's New York."

"Where does your brother live?"

"Salt Lake City," said the customer, "or just outside it."

"There's a lot of skiing out there isn't there?" Claude asked. "Do they ski?"

"Oh, yeah," the customer smiled, "everybody out there skis."

"Do you think they would like one of these hooded sweatshirts? They're great for walking in the cold and we have them in men's and women's sizes. What sizes do you need?"

"Oh, I guess he'd want an extra large and she would wear a small." The customer was looking at the sweatshirts Claude was putting on the counter. "I like this one for my brother and, let's see, this one for my sister-in-law. Thanks for your help."

Claude looked at the man as if he had forgotten his pants. "What are you and your wife gonna' be wearing?"

The customer was taken aback. "What do you mean?"

"Wouldn't it mean more to your brother if you had a shirt similar to his? If your brother thinks you like the shirt enough to wear one yourself, he'll appreciate his more. And your sister-in-law won't worry about whether she's in style if your wife's wearing one as well. See what I mean?"

"Well, maybe you're right. Give me two more shirts."

"You'll need an extra large, what color do you want, red or black?"

"I'll take a red one."

"What size and color will your wife want?"

"Let me have the blue one in a small," the man said.

Again, the cash register receipt was nearly twice what the average receipt had been.

Three days later Claude was having dinner with Bruce and Amy. They were celebrating Bruce's promotion at Genre. He would now be in charge of marketing the entire line of young men's clothes.

Bruce monopolized the conversation during dinner at Stein's Deli. Amy occasionally got in a word or two, mostly to congratulate Bruce and probe about what additional perks he would be getting. Neither of them seemed interested in how well Claude was doing selling shirts at NY/NY. Claude didn't object, though, since Bruce was picking up the tab for dinner. Claude just ate and listened.

Bruce explained in great detail how he had planned his climb up the corporate ladder, and he described the changes he would make immediately in the line. He said Genre had done well in the past but their designs were out of step with the market. He would set new records for the young men's line at Genre. He did not know about Claude's record-setting performance at his store.

Meanwhile, a couple of thousand miles away in Salt Lake City, four people were laughing as one of them told the story about walking into a shirt shop in New York to buy a $10 T-shirt, meeting a hick from Georgia and leaving with four, thirty-dollar hooded sweatshirts. The man telling the story was George Walker, the marketing director for Lucky Lad, one of Genre's major competitors.

George's brother said, "It sounds like that guy at the shirt store could teach your people a thing or two."

George smiled and winked and said, "Maybe so."

CHAPTER FIVE

Non-Retailing

If you are the owner of a retail store and sometimes you think your salespeople are doing everything they can to chase off your customers, you're probably right. However, before you decide to fire them and find some super salespeople to replace them, I would suggest that you are the one who taught them and encouraged them to do the one thing that stops people from buying. I call it non-retailing because it's an activity whose results are the opposite of what you want.

Non-retailing is so prevalent that after reading this chapter you will be able to go into any store and observe it. In fact, you will find it difficult to go into a retail outlet and not see it. It's another conditioned quirk of human nature which can be managed with effective questioning.

The following scenario will sound familiar to anyone who has shopped in a retail store in North America.

You walk into a retail establishment and begin looking at the merchandise. A "salesperson" walks up to you and says, "May I help you?" Then you say, "No thanks, just looking." Right?

Why do we do that?

For some reason, retail salespeople are taught to greet a customer with, "May I help you?" First, it's a stupid question. A salesperson's whole purpose is to help. Of course you can help, but what you really want to know is how your customer thinks you can help. Second, customers have conditioned themselves not to respond to that question, so nine times out of ten it isn't going to work.

Suppose you're on your way to buy a specific item in a certain store. Consciously or subconsciously you play the "May I help you?/No thanks, just looking" scenario through in your mind before you ever reach the store. We go through this in our mind as a result of past experience. It virtually always happens this way, because saying, "No thanks, just looking" is the verbal equivalent of pulling a gun on the salesperson. When a salesperson hears that, there is a rapid retreat to some obscure place until the customer leaves or, rarely, is ready to buy.

This behavior is even more deeply a part of our routine than we realize. As you walk into the store, the salesperson who is standing by the cash register reading a magazine sees you walk in and thinks, "Oh no. There's another customer. I'll go over and say, 'May I help you,' and then I'll hear, 'No thanks, just looking,' and I'll come back over here and finish reading my magazine." Then the strangest thing happens. The sales clerk comes over to you as you browse, says, "May I help you?" you respond, "No thanks, just looking," and the clerk leaves you alone.

I'm convinced that we have so thoroughly preprogrammed this scenario in our minds, so completely etched it into our thinking and behavior patterns, that the clerk could actually come over to us and say, "Did you know your fly was open?" and we would respond, "No thanks, just looking!"

Some of my retail clients have reported sales increases of seventeen percent or more in the first thirty days after changing this scenario. One chain of stores advised its employees that they were subject to discipline up to and including dismissal if they ever greeted a customer with the dreaded, "May I help you?" They were encouraged to use a question at the beginning of their encounter with the customer, but it couldn't be that one.

The next thing the salespeople wanted to know was what question they *could* ask. You might imagine that once they inquired, we used the opportunity to teach questioning techniques. I would rather salespeople, especially retail salespeople, develop their own questions rather than use rote questions from a book.

Never Take Money From A Stranger

The way we determine what we're going to ask is to ask ourselves, "What do I want to know?"

Now hold that thought while I explain an important principle about sales: never take money from a stranger. If someone walked up to you on the street and offered you three thousand dollars, would you take it? Would you be afraid there might be some serious ramifications if you did? Would you wonder what the other person wanted in return? When we sell to someone we don't know, we are taking money from a stranger. We shouldn't be doing that.

As salespeople, we must know the buyers' motivation. Are they buying because they need something or because they want something? What problem are they trying to solve? How much is that problem costing them and what would the solution be worth to them? Until we know these things we do not know the buyer or what the buyer wants or is willing to pay. How can we possibly sell to them?

Selling to strangers is common, even in your own home and even if it's only been three hours since you got a phone. Telemarketing has become such a successful sales technique that more and more companies have come to use it. Unfortunately, too many of them are still using the same old, tired techniques, and the typical consumer tends to tune them out immediately.

When I answer the telephone and someone says, "Mr. Reaves, how are you today?" the first thing that goes through my mind is that somebody's trying to sell me something. The fact that they call me by name is admirable, but it certainly doesn't mean that they know me. So I say, "Too busy to talk to any salespeople," and that usually chases them off. However, how do you think most people respond? "Fine."

Telemarketing people, like the rest of us, have conditioned themselves to ask how you're doing, pause and not listen, and then go into their spiel. No matter what you say, they will say, "Great. I'd like to tell you about . . . ." When that happens, I ask *them* a question. Why?

The next time you get a telephone solicitor on the line, especially one who's right out of college and wants to tell you how to invest your life savings, ask this question: "What do I do for a living?" You will probably hear stammering for a minute, and then the voice will say, "I don't know," or will ask you what you do for a living. Do you answer? Of course not, you ask another question! "If you don't even know what I do for a living how could you possibly know how to invest my money?" Or, "If you don't even know what I do for a living, how could you possibly know whether or not I need your product or service?"

When you know the people you want to sell to, they will give you more of their money. How do we get to know them? We ask them questions.

TIP #13

There are only three reasons why anyone ever buys anything, and price isn't one of them.

Keep in mind that there are only three reasons why anyone ever buys anything: they want it, they need it, or they like the salesperson. In none of these cases is price an issue. If you are having a problem getting the right price for your product, you are probably trying to take money from a stranger.

If you want something badly enough, or need something badly enough, what will you pay to have it? Price is rarely the issue. Suppose I was standing in front of you holding a twenty foot square waterproof tarpaulin, and I wanted $100 for it. Would you buy it? Not if you don't want or need it. However, suppose you arrive home tonight to find a tree has blown over causing a hole in your roof, and a storm cloud is blowing in. Now I show up and my tarpaulin is $200. Do you buy? Of course you do, because there is a clearly defined need to have the tarp.

Complete the following sentences:

Imagine that you just won the lottery and you could have anything you want. What is the one thing you've wanted for awhile?

I want ____________________________________

Now what is the one thing that you've needed for awhile?

I need ____________________________________

Now, go back and attach a dollar figure to what you wrote in the "want" statement and then attach a dollar figure to what you wrote in the "need" statement. Most people will attach a higher dollar figure to satisfying the want than to meeting the need.

How does the retail salesperson use this information? *To satisfy a desire, people will pay more; to satisfy a need, people will pay quickly.* If it's something we want, we will pay whatever we can afford, and then some. We want what we want and we want the best we can find. Something we need is usually a more urgent matter, but not nearly as romantic or interesting, so we only pay what we must.

As an example, people who sell tires sell differently to men than they do to women. For men tires are interesting. They want the latest, double steel belted, raised letter, super premium, 75,000 mile tire. Women would rather not spend money on tires at all, and will buy only what it takes to do the job. For men, tires are excitement. Women *need* tires, and they want the purchase to be as painless as possible. Tires are not advertised with the society and fashion news, they're advertised in the sports section to appeal to readers who want them. People who need them will come in anyway.

On the other hand, have you ever noticed where clothes are advertised? Even the menswear is advertised in or near the women's sections. Why? Women *want* clothes, men *need* them. Even though most men want to look good, they see clothing as a necessity. Once they find something they like, they stick with it. When their shoes wear out they go back to the same store where they bought the last pair and say, "I need another pair of shoes just like these." A salesperson who hears the word "need" knows that the sale is a done deal. Very little actual selling will be necessary, and that customer is going to leave with a pair of shoes.

The typical woman has many pairs of shoes. She enters the store and says, "I want to see this shoe in my size." The salesperson knows this customer will buy out of want, and that the sale is contingent on the woman liking the shoes, liking the way they make her ankle and leg look, liking the style and the color. Some selling is still needed here. The salesperson knows to say things like, "That looks really nice on you." If the woman likes that shoe she is likely also to buy another pair in a different color, and perhaps even another in a different style. When people buy on desire, they buy more.

Another interesting quirk of human nature is that people will confuse their wants and needs. They use the word "need" when they really mean "want." When I ask people in my seminars to fill in the blanks on the want and need questions, usually someone will put down that they need a new car. I ask them if they currently own a car that runs and they acknowledge that they do. All a car is supposed to do is take us from point A to point B, and an old car will do that. What they mean is that they want a new car. Others will write down that they need some new clothes. I ask them if they own the clothes they are wearing and when they acknowledge that they do, they are also acknowledging that they don't *need* new clothes.

Smart people don't argue with the customer's reason for buying, even if it is in error. When someone confuses a "want" with a "need," the salesperson has the best of both worlds. Since buyers will pay a lot to satisfy a want, and they will pay quickly to satisfy a need, when they say they "need" something that they actually "want," they will buy a lot of it and they will buy quickly.

Would you believe that people will actually walk into a luxury car dealership and use the word "need?" When a person walks into a Cadillac dealership and says, "I need a new Cadillac," the salesperson will walk them past the DeVille line and take them over to the Fleetwood Broughams. The customer has confused "wants" with "needs," and the alert salesperson will bypass the less expensive line to show what the customer truly *wants*.

The Salesperson Is Everything

Still, it all hinges on the salesperson. Even if we want something badly enough, even if we need it, we will go out of our way to do business with someone else if we don't like the salesperson. There is usually another company that can supply anything we want. However, most sales usually boil down to an individual buyer making a purchase from an individual salesperson. Companies don't do business with companies, people do business with people.

For instance, how many people do you know who need Girl Scout Cookies? OK, except for the Chocolate Mint, how many people do you know who need Girl Scout Cookies? How many people even want them? If they were in such high demand wouldn't they be in the stores beside the Oreo cookies? But when the doorbell rings and we open it to find that little cherub face looking back at us, what do we do? We buy! Not one box, usually we buy several boxes.

When the purchase is more frequent and more costly than Girl Scout Cookies, we become more serious about our buying habits. We want to buy from someone we think knows what we want, or understands what we need, someone who has taken the time to get to know us. After all, sometimes we do not really know what we want or need, and when someone takes the time to help us sort it out, we appreciate it. We go back to them for subsequent purchases because we feel they are making the effort to know us. They ask their questions and they listen to our answers.

If a man goes into a hardware store and asks for a quarter-inch drill bit, what does he want? He wants a quarter-inch hole. The only way he knows to get the hole is to buy the bit, take it home, put it in his drill and drill the hole. Now, what if the hardware store sold holes? When the man said, "I need a quarter-inch drill bit," couldn't the sales clerk have said, "Don't you really want a quarter-inch hole?" The customer would say, "Yes," and then the clerk could say, "Here's one! Take it home and plug it in and you have a hole!"

Now you may think that's absurd, but it happened to me. Several years ago I bought my first refrigerator with an ice maker. I was excited. In the middle of the summer, I would have ice. No more sloshing trays of water all over the kitchen, just open the doors, I thought, and there would be the ice.

I devoted a Saturday to installing the ice maker. Early that morning I went down to the basement with pencil, paper and tape measure. I was living in a house that had galvanized plumbing. If you've ever worked with galvanized pipes you know it's a job that involves injuring knuckles, shedding blood and losing one's temper.

I went to the hardware store with my list and said to the sales clerk, "I need three feet and five inches of half-inch galvanized pipe, threaded on both ends. I need another piece of half-inch galvanized pipe, two feet and six and a half inches, also threaded on both ends. I need a tee connector, a cut off valve, a reducer, copper tubing, fittings. . . ." The clerk interrupted me and asked, "What are you trying to do, put in an ice maker?" I said, "Yes." He said, "You don't need most of that stuff," and he sold me the equivalent of a hole. It was something called a saddle valve and I had never heard of it. I took it home, clamped it on a pipe, turned off the water, drilled a hole, put the fittings on and turned on the water. I had planned to spend the entire day in the basement installing the ice maker. I had already planned to call a plumber on Monday morning to straighten out the mess I made in the basement on Saturday. Instead, thanks to an alert sales clerk, I was done in forty-five minutes.

I have since moved away from the neighborhood, but I always go back to that store. I drive past the national chains, past other mom-and-pop hardware stores, and make my way over to the one where the salespeople know how to ask questions and know how to listen.

We need to know the customer's need or desire. All too often we learn that they don't know what they really want or need. I thought I needed a lot of plumbing supplies when all I really needed was a device I had never seen. The clerk could have said, "Do you want the high-grade galvanized pipe or the contractor grade," and I would have chosen one. Either way it would not have been the best solution to my problem. By asking what I was trying to accomplish, the clerk was able to help me solve the problem, not just address the symptoms.

When constructing questions keep in mind that you want to know the buyer's criteria for making the purchase, and you also want them to like you. As you start to formulate the opening and follow-up questions you will use, assess whether they can stand the test: are they positioning you with the customer and helping you determine what the customer wants?

Keep in mind that most purchases are made to solve a real or a perceived problem. The greater the problem, the greater the probability of sale. The more problems a purchase will solve, the greater the probability of sale. Identifying the problem positions the salesperson. Quantifying the problem makes the sale easier to close. After all, if a $50 purchase will solve a $5,000 problem, the customer is likely to buy quickly.

The Story Continues . . .

Claude was having the time of his life. His apartment was now complete, the occasional bonuses he received from Bill, the owner of NY/NY, added to the quality of his lifestyle. Most of all, he enjoyed what he was doing. He really couldn't understand why some people said they didn't like sales.

On a cold Wednesday afternoon, a familiar face entered NY/NY right at closing time. The man approached Claude.

"Do you remember me?"

Claude thought for a minute, studied the man's face and answered, "Oh, yeah. You're the guy with kin folks in Salt Lake City. How'd they like their sweatshirts?"

"Somehow I thought you'd remember," the man chuckled. "They liked them fine. In fact, I came by to, uh, to ..." At that moment the man noticed Bill walking into the store from the back room. "They liked them so much," he continued, "that I'd like to take you to dinner tonight. Could you do that?"

"Sure," Claude said with a big smile, "but that's not necessary."

"It's no problem. What time is good for you?"

Claude answered, "I get off in thirty minutes. Any time after that is fine."

"Good. I'll pick you up out front in thirty minutes. My name is George Walker." The man reached out to shake hands with Claude.

"Claude. Claude Thompson."

The men shook hands and Walker left. Thirty minutes later a light gray limousine was standing at the curb outside of NY/NY. When Claude left the store and locked the door, he heard George Walker's voice behind him.

"Let's eat, Claude!" Claude turned and saw George standing on the curb behind the open rear door of the limo. George waved his hand and pointed to the inside of the car. Once inside it was obvious to George that Claude had never been in such a grand automobile before.

"What kind of food do you like, Claude?"

"Actually, I'm partial to country cookin'," Claude said, "but there ain't much of that in New York. Anywhere you'd like to go is fine."

George smiled, pressed a button on his door and the glass partition behind the chauffeur came down. "Malcolm, Claude here likes country cooking. What do you think?"

Malcolm was a large, black man in his early forties with steely eyes and a warm, genuine grin. "I think it's time to visit Mary's."

"Sounds good to me. Call her and see if she has a special table available."

Malcolm smiled and nodded. The glass partition went back up and Claude could see Malcolm talking on the phone as he drove.

The conversation between George and Claude focused mainly on Claude's story, . . . how he managed to find himself in New York and how he learned to sell. Claude had just begun to tell George about the apartment when the car pulled up at the curb in front of a small, simple looking restaurant. Over the door was an old and fading sign that said, "Mary's."

Inside the atmosphere was not typically "New York." A few patrons waited for tables while the servers took care of their diners without seeming rushed at all. Mary's was a quiet place, old but clean, and people who ate there were dressed in everything from suits to utility company uniforms.

In a moment a large black woman with mostly gray hair and a big smile walked out of the kitchen, waved at George and said, "Mr. Walker, your party's back here. I'll show you." Then, with a quick glance at Claude, she led the two men to a back room. It looked like someone's dining room. There were windows that looked out on an alley and the room was furnished with a dining room suite that was complete down to the doilies on the backs of the chairs.

"Enjoy your dinner," the lady said, "I'll check in on you in a minute."

"That was Mary," George said.

As soon as the men were seated, George asked Claude to continue telling him about his adventures in New York. They were only occasionally interrupted by a waiter who took their drink orders and brought a basket of bread. By the time Claude had finished his story the table was covered with large bowls of vegetables, plates with chicken, beef and catfish on them and a large pitcher of iced tea.

"This looks great," Claude said. "I didn't know such food could be found here. I gotta' remember this place."

"I thought you'd like it, Claude." The men were passing bowls to each other and heaping food onto their plates. "So your cousin Bruce works for Genre. What does he do?"

"I'm not exactly sure. It's some kind of marketing job, he said. I think it's mostly in the boy's clothes."

"Is he the one who taught you how to sell?"

"Bruce? No. He's too important to sell. He has an office and stuff like that. In fact, I don't think he knows a whole lot about selling."

"So who taught you, Claude?"

"Well, actually it just sorta' happened. Angie didn't come to work one day and I was the only one in the store when some customers came in, and I just tried to help them as best I could. So I wasn't really selling so much as I was just helpin'."

George grinned.

"What's so funny?" Claude asked.

"That's the message I've been trying to get through to my salespeople for years." George was shaking his head. "Claude, I think I want you to join my team. I'm head of the sales department for Lucky Lad. Have you ever heard of us?"

"I think I've seen some of your ads on the sides of buses."

"That's us. We have a full line of boys' and young men's clothes. We're expanding into men's, girls' and misses'. We're going to have a line of athletic shoes, designer socks and even jewelry. Not only that, we're about to open our own stores in malls all over the country!" It was obvious that George was excited about what Lucky Lad was doing. "I think you could help us develop our retail marketing strategy."

"I don't think so, Mr. Walker," Claude said.

"Please, Claude, call me George. Why not? Pass the mashed potatoes, would you?"

"Mostly because I don't even know what that is. You need a smart person like Bruce for that. You want some gravy, too?"

"Please. What I mean is that you could teach us how to sell more effectively in our stores. You would show our people how you sell, and we would teach them the specifics about our products. I want our people to learn how to sell like you do." George was pointing his fork at Claude as he spoke.

The two men ate in silence for a few moments and then Claude asked, "Don't your people already know how to sell?"

George smiled and said, "Yes, of course. But they sell like everybody else. If we're going to have the kind of impact in the market that I think we can, we're going to have to do better. Whatever it is that you're doing, that's what I call better."

"I don't know about teaching. I didn't do that well in school, I can't imagine myself teaching. Besides, I'm kinda' shy, I'd feel real nervous in front of a room full of people." As Claude spoke George could sense that he was becoming more reticent about accepting the new position.

"How about this, Claude. You teach our training personnel and they'll teach the others. How would that be?" George wasn't sure that what he was proposing would work but he was mostly concerned about getting Claude on his team.

Claude said, "I'll have to sleep on it. I'll let you know."

George wasn't ready to give up. "Claude, the position pays thirty-five thousand dollars a year. You'll have your own office, not a large one, of course, but an office. You'll have the chance to travel, so there'll be an expense account." As he spoke, George watched Claude's eyes to see if any of those things caused any reaction. The salary seemed to have done it, so he knew what his next question should be. "How much are you making now, Claude?"

"Not as much as you're talking about!" Claude's face went from a large smile to a concerned look all in about ten seconds. "Wait a minute. Is this legal?"

George put down his fork, laughed, looked at Claude and said, "Look. I don't know who you're working for now. I do know that he has the best deal on an employee in New York and he probably knows it too. You're worth a lot more than you're being paid. Frankly, in your boss' position I would probably do the same thing: I'd pay you only what you asked for. The fact is, Claude, I think you're worth more than thirty-five thousand dollars to Lucky Lad, but I believe I can entice you to join us with that salary."

Claude thought for a minute and then said, "So, you think that people pay only what they have to for things, not what things are actually worth?"

"Exactly."

Claude grinned, "Then to hire me you're gonna' have to pay forty thousand dollars."

"Are you kidding? I'm offering you the chance of a life-time!"

"Yeah, I know. I was just testing your theory."

"Then we have a deal?" George asked.

"Deal!" Claude reached out his hand.

As the two men shook hands, George said, "I would have paid forty."

Claude smiled and said, "I would have taken thirty."

When Mary brought the desserts, Malcolm came in, sat down at the table and asked, "Did he go for it?"

George said, "Malcolm, meet the newest member of our team!"

Claude was a little confused. "You mean you guys had this all set up?"

"Of course," George said. "Look, Claude, Malcolm and I are a lot like you. We treat everybody as equals except those hot shots who think they know it all. You're what we call 'good people' and you're an excellent salesperson. Do you remember Malcolm coming into your store?"

"Well, I meet a lot of people, you know. I can't say I remember him."

"Good. I sent him in to spy on you, to watch you sell. He saw the same talent I did. That's why you're here."

Claude looked at Malcolm. "But I thought you were the chauffeur."

"I am," Malcolm said.

George interrupted, "Actually, Malcolm is officially compensated for being the chauffeur. He's really as much a part of the team as anyone else. We all work together. This restaurant belongs to Malcolm's mother. Mary runs this place. I know that we can eat here, have our privacy and get a great meal. Oh, how was your dinner, by the way?"

"Wonderful. Almost like home cooking."

George continued, "Tonight the hot shots are across town spending hundreds of dollars on an expensive dinner that isn't nearly as good. We ate like kings, Mary makes a good profit and everybody wins. That's what teamwork is all about. And now you're a part of the team."

Back in his apartment, Claude couldn't sleep. He was too excited about the new job, a little scared that it might not work, and apprehensive about telling Bill he would be leaving. He had tried to call Bruce for advice, but when he heard the answering machine he remembered that Bruce would be out of town for several weeks.

As usual, when he needed help in making a decision, he opened up the red notebook that Larry had given him in Clarkesville, and found some advice. He read, "Everything worth having involves risk. Nothing great comes to us without it."

Claude thought about what George had said, that Claude was a part of his team. It didn't make his decision any easier since the ultimate responsibility was his. Claude made another entry:

**Risk belongs to individuals,
victories belong to teams.**

CHAPTER SIX

The Only Question You'll Ever Have To Answer

When you can answer one single question, people will buy whatever you're selling, people will give you things, people will give you their time, people will introduce you to others, people will open doors for you that you never dreamed existed.

So, your question is, "What's the question?" The only question you ever have to answer, and you must be able to answer it, is,

What's In It For Me?

In the sales world this is commonly known as the WIIFM. It is important to go beyond what you may have already learned about WIIFM, to understand how powerful it can be.

The basic premise of WIIFM is that people don't buy things, they buy what things can do. Once we understand what a product is wanted for, we can sell that item. However, the reason one person buys something is not the same reason everybody else buys it. In other words, everyone wants something different, even though they are all buying identical things. We need to understand what people want and then convince them that what we have will satisfy their needs.

For instance, suppose you sell ball point pens. In fact, imagine that you sell Mont Blanc pens, which are very high quality and retail for about $100. How would you sell that pen? After all, the purpose of having a pen is to write, and a thirty-nine cent plastic pen will do that very nicely. Why would anyone buy the $100 Mont Blanc?

Here's where the feature-benefit analysis once worked. Please notice the use of the phrase, "once worked."

In the feature-benefit analysis, we make a list of all the features of our product or service. Then, for each of those features, we make a list of benefits. When we talk to the customer, we talk benefits not features.

That used to work. Suppose we came up with ten features for our product and, for each of those features, we identified ten benefits. We would then have 100 benefits. We would go out and hit the customer over the head with all 100 benefits, hoping that at least one of them would hit home. We were saying, "Here's 100 reasons for giving me your money, pick one!"

Now, to this process, we have added two crucial steps. First, we tie the benefits to solutions and, second, we tie the solutions to the customer's problem(s). We begin by asking ourselves, "What solutions does this benefit offer?" Once we know what solutions we have to offer, we ask our customers what problems they have and match our solutions to the customers' problems.

Let's go back to the ball point pen, and list its features.

Retractable Point
Clip
Replaceable Cartridge
It Writes
14K Gold Trim

We want to sell our Mont Blanc pen for $100. How would we do it? Without *asking*, we would *tell* the customer about the features. Now imagine that you are the salesperson and imagine that your potential customer is standing across the counter with a pen that cost $1.00. Using the features we listed, if we said that our pen has a retractable point, the customer would push the button on top of the $1.00 pen and operate the retractable point. If we pointed out our pen's clip, we would be shown the clip on the plastic pen. If we mentioned the replaceable cartridge and the fact that it writes, the customer could show us those same features on the $1.00 pen. We could mention the 14K gold trim on our pen, knowing that the plastic pen does not have that. However, we have established that there is no functional difference between the two pens; they only differ in appearance. The customer is unlikely to see that as a $99 difference.

On the other hand, suppose we had begun our presentation with a question like, "Is appearance important to you?" If the customer answered positively, we would try to sell our pen based on its appearance, and maybe we would succeed. If we didn't, we would have little to fall back on since appearance was the only feature that differentiated our pen from the customer's pen. Selling on features is a risky, usually unsuccessful technique.

Because selling features presented problems, someone years ago came up with the idea of changing features into benefits and selling benefits. Some called it "selling the sizzle instead of the steak." Using that method, we would sit down with our list of features and expand it to include a list of benefits for each feature. The list for our $100 pen might look like this:

Features	**Benefits**
Retractable Point	Won't mar clothes
	Point won't be damaged
	Avoid unintentional marks
	Point won't dry out, clog
Clip	Pen stays put, can be found
	Pen won't fall out, won't be damaged
	Pen won't roll away
	Pen can be used to keep papers together
Replaceable Cartridge	Saves money, buy refill, not pen
	Same pen, multiple colors
	Extend life of pen

It Writes	Will sign purchase orders
	Records important data
	Portable data recorder
	Can leave important information for others
	Will sign checks
14K Gold Trim	Improves user's image
	Indication of quality
	Less likely to forget it

Using feature-benefit analysis, we now have 19 reasons a customer would want to buy our pen. Some people stop now, thinking they have the answer to WIIFM, but they don't. What they have are reasons for buying that apply to the masses. They are in a position to answer the question, "What's in it for *us*?" but they haven't focused on the reasons that a specific customer might want our Mont Blanc pen. That's because they have not tied a specific benefit to the solution of a customer's specific problem.

By doing the basic feature-benefit analysis and asking a few questions, the alert pen salesperson can sell the $100 pen to the user of the plastic pen. The techniques might include the Three-Question Technique, the Built-In Assumption technique, and maybe even the $75,000 Question technique. The conversation might go something like this:

> SALESPERSON: "What type of pen are you currently using?"

> CUSTOMER: "I use these plastic pens."

> SALESPERSON: What is your criteria for choosing the pen you use?" (Note: "Why are you using plastic pens?" is a "why/you" question, that would have put the customer on the defensive.)

> CUSTOMER: "They're cheap."

> SALESPERSON: "Is that important?"

> CUSTOMER: "Yes, it saves money, and a pen is a pen."

SALESPERSON: "I see. What happens when it runs out of ink?"

CUSTOMER: "I buy another one just like it. Another dollar."

SALESPERSON: "How often does that happen?"

CUSTOMER: "Well, actually, not very often. I usually lose the pen before it runs out of ink."

SALESPERSON: "Tell me about a time when you lost your pen and needed it, does one episode stand out?"

CUSTOMER: "Not really. I might answer the phone and someone starts giving me a lot of numbers or something and I realize I can't find my pen. It's mostly just a short-term aggravation."

SALESPERSON: "For whom?"

CUSTOMER: "Well, for me. Oh, yeah, and for the other person, I suppose."

SALESPERSON: "How does a pen get lost? Doesn't it have a clip?"

CUSTOMER: "Yes, but the clip is part of the cap and when I take the cap off to write, the clip goes with it."

SALESPERSON: "How else does your pen disappear?"

CUSTOMER: "Well, sometimes I walk off and leave it somewhere. You know how it is."

SALESPERSON: "Do the pens ever seem to disappear from your desk magically?"

CUSTOMER: "Well, sometimes people borrow them and I never see them again, if that's what you mean."

SALESPERSON: "If I could show you a pen that was of such high quality that it would outlast dozens of the refills you put in it, one that has a permanent, tight clip on it so you wouldn't lose it, and one that is so distinctive that everyone would know whose pen it is even if you mislaid it, would you be interested?"

CUSTOMER: "Perhaps."

Show the customer the pen and then ask this version of the $75,000 Question, "What do you like most about this pen?" If the answer is something like, "I like the gold trim," the customer is buying a feature. If you hear, "I like the idea that I'm not as likely to lose it," the customer is buying a benefit. The difference is that an expensive item is more likely to be sold based on benefits than on features.

Suppose you're not selling a product, but you're a manager and you want to make something happen in your organization. For example, you want to hire a new secretary and you need the approval of your boss. To get the approval, you must address the question that will be in the back of the boss' mind: WIIFM. Even if the boss does not ask directly, stating how the new secretary will benefit the boss will increase the likelihood of your getting what you want.

You can state, "I need a new secretary," and see what happens. Or you can list all of the features of having a new secretary: the ability to turn out more work and to do it faster. Or you can list the benefits of each of those features: higher productivity means greater revenue; responding quickly means happier customers; doing more things means a greater competitive edge.

However, even that is not as thorough as we might be in answering WIIFM. Whether we're selling pens or asking for a new secretary, we need to turn those benefits into solutions to the customer's problem(s).

Notice that we are talking about the *customer's* problems. If the customer does not perceive something to be a problem, then it isn't one. If you think something is a problem and the customer does not see it that way, the first thing you have to sell is the idea that a problem exists. How do you do that? With questions, of course.

An established family business with which I worked had a powerful grandfather at the top of the organization chart. This gentleman ruled with an iron fist using the same management techniques his father had used in the 1920s. He didn't view that as a problem, even though his attrition rate at the time was over forty percent. If he didn't like an individual for any reason, that person was fired. There were lawsuits over the arbitrary dismissals, morale at the workplace was low, and people stole from the company just to "get even with the old man." Still, he did not see his management style as a problem.

We sat in his office and he gave me the initial overview of what was wrong at his company. The main problem was the company's employees, and that virtually everyone in the company was wrong except him. After he had completed this monologue, I asked some questions.

"What would you like for your company to accomplish over the next three years?" This question, asked three times in three different ways, elicited a laundry list of new products, new markets and higher profits.

"What three things are standing between you and each of your goals?" This one took awhile to answer but, after pointing a finger at everyone in the company, he finally admitted that perhaps a little of the problem could be coming from his own office.

"How would you do things differently if . . .," was the next question, using several different "ifs." Then, to help him identify his areas of weakness, I asked, "What are the three most important traits of a leader?"

Notice that the phrasing of the questions significantly reduced their threat. That made it easy for us to discuss issues instead of personalities or individuals. The key was that we had established up front what was in it for him by having him list his goals and dreams. By following this non-threatening format, we were able to define the customer's problems in a way that he could acknowledge later on.

The next step is to quantify the problems, an important step in the WIIFM scenario. The more your idea is worth to the other person, the greater your value is to them. It is important that the other person do the quantification, but we can assist their thinking.

"What would you be doing with your time if you were not spending it on this issue?" "What would you do with your money if it wasn't being spent on this effort?" Notice that this line of questioning goes beyond simple cost quantification. Instead of asking, "What is this costing you?" we ask what they would be doing with the money if it was not being spent on this problem. This more closely addresses the WIIFM question, because it shows what they *could* have if they did not have the problem. It also shows them what they *will* have when the problem is solved.

We often make the erroneous assumption that once we do the quantification, other people will naturally see the correlation. They may not see at first that spending less on solving problems will give them funds to invest in more productive areas. They might not recognize immediately that spending less time putting out fires would free them to do the things they've wanted to do.

My client and I identified several new products, one new process, and a new venture he wanted to pursue. By solving the problems he identified, he would have the time and the funds to make those new, exciting and potentially lucrative things happen. In other words, we satisfied the issue of what would be in it for him.

Remember that just because someone asks you a question doesn't mean you have to answer it. It's more important to understand the question than to respond to it. When you are asked a question, ask yourself, "What do they really want to know?"

Years ago, when sixty-second commercials were the norm, the following commercial ran on television. A man returns from a business trip and is met at the airport by his wife and kids. As they drive home, the wife says,

> "The roses died."
> The husband asks, "How did they die?"
> She says, "It must have been the heat."
> "The heat," he says, "this is winter! What heat?"
> "From the garage," she says.

"Why would the garage have heat?"

"It was on fire," she answers.

"How did the garage catch on fire?" Now the husband is getting excited.

"The firemen think it was probably a spark from the house."

Notice the line of questioning and how it led to the essential information. The wife did not want to alarm the husband, so she started with a less threatening statement and led him slowly to the really bad news. The husband, not particularly wanting this information, allowed himself to be led question by question.

People do that all the time. Most of us prefer to avoid confrontation, which means that most of us choose not to ask WIIFM, even though we really want to know before we make a decision. To succeed, it's important to keep in mind that people often have an agenda that's hidden in the questions they ask.

When I say to my children, "How much do you love me?" they realize it's our family "code" and they know I'm about to ask a favor. Immediately their minds begin working on what could be in it for them. When they ask me for money, I ask them point blank, WIIFM. They usually try to get by with something like, "My undying love and affection," and I usually don't let them get away with it.

If my son offers to wash and wax my car in exchange for having the use of it on prom night, I may or may not be interested. If he begins by *asking* me how much I pay to have my car waxed, he knows he has started with a quantified WIIFM. He might also approach me with the questions, "How many hours does it take you to wash and wax your car?" followed by, "What would you do with those hours if someone took care of those chores for you?" Now my son has a quantified WIIFM whose value is clear to me.

Delta Airlines understands the WIIFM scenario. I have a million miles with them because they keep asking for my business, I keep asking WIIFM and they keep answering. Actually, I never had a conversation with a representative from Delta on this subject, but they learned what I wanted from customer surveys, they watched what other carriers were doing, and they tried to make every encounter a positive one.

Every time we fly we have a choice. We can fly or drive or take the train. When we choose to fly we have options: different carriers, different times, even different routes. Since all of the airlines buy their airplanes from the same companies, their only distinction is service. Successful airlines are the ones which are constantly asking, "What's in it for our customers?" Failing carriers are the ones which are constantly asking, "What's in it for us?" Being able to answer the customer's WIIFM is critical to staying in business.

Successful managers always ask what their directives will mean to their subordinates. Successful salespeople habitually put themselves in their customer's position. Great parents think through their children's motivation before asking their offspring to do something.

When my first book was about to be published, I called a prominent figure in business and asked him to read it and give me a quote for the dust jacket. I knew that *I* would be flattered if someone asked me to do that, and I erroneously assumed he would feel the same way. He stopped me cold when he asked, "Why should I do that?" I was totally unprepared, stammered and then responded, "It would give you national exposure."

His next question really threw me. "Why would I want that?" I thought everybody wanted to be famous. Everybody likes to see their name in print, right? Not this guy. I never did get a quote from him, but I learned from that encounter to have an answer to the WIIFM before approaching anyone for anything.

Someone once figured out that each of us is only four people away from anyone else in the world. In other words, if you wanted to reach someone, say the President of the United States, you already know someone who knows someone who knows someone who knows that person. If you can answer the WIIFM question at every step, with each person, you can be introduced to, or have your message carried to the President.

I have seen this happen very often. People who are neither extraordinary nor well connected find a way to get in to see whomever they want. They receive things others only dream of—advice, help, material things, even money. You can have these things, too, in any area of your life, IF

You Know What You Want,
You Know What The Other Person Wants,
and
YOU ASK FOR IT!

The Story Concludes . . .

For Claude it was like a dream. He had his own office and a secretary. He had a parking space which he never used because he didn't have a car. His one problem was that he wasn't exactly sure what he was supposed to be doing.

The only person who discouraged Claude was his cousin. Bruce couldn't believe that Claude had landed in the kind of job he was describing. However, Lucky Lad was known for breaking all the conventional rules in design, production and advertising, so it was possible something this bizarre could happen also. There was a part of Bruce that felt protective toward his country cousin, and wanted to shelter Claude from some big-city hustler. Then there was the other side of Bruce. The side that was jealous.

George Walker had shown Claude around and had introduced him to a few people. Some of them were salespeople who would actually report to Claude, but most of the sales force worked out of regional offices around the country, and Claude would meet them at the next semi-annual sales meeting.

In the meantime, George put Claude on a fast track program to learn only as much about the garment industry as George thought was absolutely necessary. He did not want Claude thinking just like every other sales manager, so George purposely told him little about how salespeople were "typically" managed.

After a few weeks, Claude was sitting in his office when George came in and sat down. "It's time for you to start earning your keep, Claude."

"I'm ready, George. What do you want me to do?"

"Our next sales meeting is in three weeks." Claude could tell that George was excited about whatever was on his mind. "Tomorrow I want you to go shopping. I want you to shop our competitors' stores and then I want you to go shopping in our test store, the only one we have."

Claude asked, "So you want me to go meet the people in the test store?"

"That's exactly what I *don't* want you to do. Since they don't know you yet, you can go in, see how they're selling and then decide how they could sell better. George was smiling and watching Claude's reaction. "Then, at the sales meeting, you will teach our people how to sell in retail stores. Maybe our other salespeople, the ones who sell to retail chains, will learn something, too."

Claude looked apprehensive and said, "I don't know, George. I've never taught anything before."

George slapped his knee, stood up and said, "You leave that to me, Claude. I have some ideas that will make it real easy for you. Trust me."

The next day Claude and his secretary planned an agenda that would take Claude to several stores each day for three days, and then to Lucky Lad's test store.

Before leaving his office, Claude called his cousin. "Bruce, how's it going?"

"I'm a bit rushed right now, Claude. What do you need?" Claude could hear several conversations in the background.

"I need to talk with you. Could we do supper tonight?"

"Well, that's not really good for me, Claude. Amy and I were planning to go out for dinner."

"Bring her along! I haven't seen her in awhile. How about the Italian place around the corner from your apartment at, say, eight o'clock?"

Bruce hesitated for a moment, so Claude said, "It's important, Bruce."

Bruce reacted to the urgency in Claude's voice. "OK. Eight o'clock. See you there."

Over dinner Claude explained his assignment to Bruce and Amy and then said, "I don't know how to travel. You do it all the time. Tell me how."

For the next ninety minutes, Bruce and Amy told stories and gave Claude tips about how to get in and out of airports and hotels, what to watch for and how to survive on the road. They really seemed to enjoy being the "experts." Bruce asked very little about Claude's new position, and they parted company on the sidewalk in front of the restaurant.

Walking up the street Bruce said to Amy, "Now I get it. They hired Claude as a mystery shopper. They just want him to go into competitors' stores and their own stores and act like a customer. He's not really a marketing director." The two walked in silence for a few minutes. Bruce was still deep in thought. As he put the key in the door of their apartment building Bruce said, "Now it all makes sense. Yeah."

The next morning Claude was off on his adventure. The following three days were a blur of airports, hotels, malls and stores. Every night, as he compiled his notes, he noticed a distinct pattern. It seemed that every encounter in every store was virtually the same. In each store the salesperson had approached Claude and asked, "May I help you?" Claude had always said, "No thanks, I'm just looking." He had then been left alone to shop at his leisure and, when he wanted help, it was sometimes difficult to find a salesperson. He thought these circumstances were strange.

Back in New York Claude spent the better part of a day reviewing his findings with George, who was not surprised to hear what Claude had to say, nor that the Lucky Lad store was doing as poorly as the others Claude had visited. "Actually," George said, "this is pretty good news, Claude. We can see what's wrong, we know that our competitors are making the same mistakes, and we are ahead of the game because we have someone who can fix it for us."

"We do?" Claude asked. "Who?"

George seemed to ignore the question. "Claude, how would you deal with a customer in one of our stores? What would you do differently?"

"Well, first of all, I think I'd try to get to know them a little. Maybe find out what kind of activities they like, what they think is cool, you know, things like that."

George then asked, "How would you do that?"

Claude did not even have to think. "You just start asking them about themselves. Folks always like talking about themselves."

"And then what?"

"Then you find out what they really want, show them some things and if they like something, they buy it."

"Could you teach our salespeople how to do that, Claude?"

"I could talk to them about it. I don't know how good a teacher I'd be. But I think it'd be better if we had that person who you said could fix things for us to teach our salespeople, don't you?"

George smiled. "The sales conference starts Monday. Come with me down to the display room. I want to show you something."

The display room was set up to look like the interior of a retail store. It was complete down to the last detail, including a cash register. There were racks and shelves of clothing and accessories, and a few point-of-sale pieces and other signage.

George looked at Claude and asked, "How do you like it? This is our 'classroom.'"

"It's nice," Claude said looking around, "it looks like a real store."

"That was the idea. We wanted a place where we could test our merchandising, store layouts and things like that. So we built this. It also seems like the best place for you to show our salespeople how to sell."

"What do you mean?"

George began walking through the racks as he spoke.

"We'll bring the salespeople in, let a couple of them play the role of customers and you'll try to sell to them. The other salespeople will observe. When you've completed the transaction, the salespeople will discuss what they saw."

"So I just have to act like this is my store and try to sell some Lucky Lad clothes to the salespeople who are acting like customers?" Claude asked.

"That's it. I think our people are sharp enough to pick up what you're doing and see how they can use your techniques."

The next day the sales conference was held in the mock store in Lucky Lad's corporate headquarters. After a few preliminary agenda items were concluded, George announced that Claude would be acting as a salesperson and some of the field salespeople could volunteer to act as customers. There were plenty of anxious volunteers. Then George introduced Claude to the group, giving as little background information on Claude as possible.

The first "customers" were two male salespeople. The other salespeople would observe, make notes and, after the "customers" left, critique the process. Claude stood by the cash register.

The two men who were posing as customers went in and began looking at the new line of men's shirts. Because one of the purposes of the meeting was to introduce the new products, this was the first time the salespeople had seen the line. The colors were brighter than the previous season's and there had been some interesting changes in the styles.

Claude watched them for a moment, then walked over to them and said, "What do you think of those colors?"

The taller of the two, a 33-year-old named Bob, spoke first. "I was just wondering if it would sell. It looks a bit garish compared to what Lucky Lad was offering last year. I don't know. . . ."

Claude had no way of knowing he was talking to the most pessimistic of Lucky Lad's salespeople. Before Claude could respond, the other "customer," Brent, also answered Claude's question.

"I was hoping to find something similar to what I

bought last year. I really liked that shirt, but it's been washed so much it doesn't look as sharp as I'd like. I want another one just like it." Brent knew that all the other salespeople were watching, and he was mugging for his audience. A slightly younger man from Dallas, Brent was learning the ropes from Bob, the pessimist.

Claude was undaunted. "You don't see anything like what you bought last year?"

"No," said Brent, "there are only all of these new shirts."

"You might be able to find what you're looking for in one of our outlet stores. That's where Lucky Lad sells off our older styles. There's one out on Long Island, do you know where it is?" Claude could play his role convincingly because he had not met either of these people before.

Brent responded, "Yes, but I don't shop at outlets."

"Why is that?" Claude asked.

"Because my image and my time are important to me. That's why I want to be able to walk into a fashionable department store, pick out what I want, pay for it and be on my way. That's the way I shop." Brent glanced at Bob as he spoke, so Bob felt obligated to speak as well.

"It's the same for me. I know what I want, I know what will sell, and these colors just don't do anything for me." Bob was using the argument that he heard most often from the department store buyers he called on. He was trying to make a point with his regional manager, who was in the audience.

Claude asked a question which was not specifically addressed to either of them. "So, you like Lucky Lad, you just don't like these colors? Is that right?"

"Yes," Bob said, "we've liked Lucky Lad in the past, but these colors are just too much." Again he was treating Claude like the buyers treated him. If this new guy, Claude, was such a hot shot, Bob wanted to put him to the test in front of everyone.

Claude continued, "What is it about Lucky Lad that you like?"

"Up until now, The Look," Brent said. He was beginning to see how he was going to be treated when he took the line into the buyers. He was picking up on Bob's attitude.

Claude wasn't letting it get to him. "Have you been buying Lucky Lad for a long time?"

"Years."

"And have you seen a lot of changes in the style over the years?"

"Yes, of course. But this is too radical."

"And style is important to you, huh?"

"Very."

Claude thought for a minute and then said, "Why would Lucky Lad change styles like this?"

"Well, they've always been the first to introduce new fads. In fact, if this stuff catches on, everybody will be using these colors next season." Bob's answer reflected some of the arguments he had used in the past.

"How often does that happen?" Claude asked.

"All the time," Bob answered.

"Well, there's your answer then," Claude said and smiled.

Bob and Brent looked at each other. It was Brent who ventured the question, "What answer?"

Claude said, "If you want last year's fashion, go look in our competitors' stores." There was some laughter in the audience. "But I thought you said that style was important to you. If the other companies are always a year behind Lucky Lad, shouldn't you stick to the leader?"

The two men looked at Claude without saying anything, so Claude continued. "What size are you?"

At this point George stood up and said, "That's good." He looked at Bob and Brent and said, "Thanks, guys, you were great." He asked the two men to sit in the audience while he and Claude sat on stools in front.

George looked at the audience and asked for a critique. In the informal give-and-take conversation that followed, most of the salespeople expressed surprise that Claude had seemed so calm. Claude told them that their comment surprised him, because he had felt so nervous during the entire role play. He went on to say that being around professional salespeople like them was intimidating to him, and having to sell to two veterans really had him scared. By the time he finished speaking, many of the salespeople liked him and all of them appreciated his candor.

George asked his salespeople, "What techniques did Claude use to overcome the objections of the customers?" The answers started immediately.

"He told them that the competitors' styles were out of date," one said.

"Yes," said another, "but first he found out that style was important to them."

"He didn't try to apologize for the colors. He never said anything negative about them."

"Right! And when they seemed satisfied, he sold them a shirt!" Some of the salespeople were more than a little impressed.

After the comments, George asked, "What basic technique did Claude use?"

The salespeople looked puzzled.

"Feature-benefit analysis?" asked one.

"Overcoming objections!" shouted someone from the back of the room.

Other salespeople ventured other responses, but they could tell from the look on his face that George wasn't hearing what he wanted to hear. After a few more guesses, George helped them out. "What did Claude *say* during his sales call?"

A young salesperson in the front row raised her hand. When George pointed to her she said, "I noticed that! He didn't *say* anything. He just asked questions."

"Right! Thank you, Debbie. Claude's approach is to keep the customer talking until he knows what the customer wants and, in this case, why the customer would want it. He does that by asking questions. His entire sales presentation was one series of questions. What was his first question?"

The salespeople were quiet for awhile, and then one said, "I know. It was 'May I help you?'"

George smiled. "Actually, it wasn't. In fact, Claude never asks that question, that's one of the things that caught my attention about him. What kind of questions does he ask?"

Again the group sat silently for awhile; they were becoming a bit gun shy. Claude was also sitting quietly, taking it all in. Finally one of them said, "I don't really remember his exact questions, but he seemed to be trying to get to know what they wanted."

"Right," George said, "he asks about *their* interests. He's able to answer the only questions our customers ever need to have answered, and that is, "What's in it for me?"

George paused a moment to let that sink in before he continued. "Claude seems to be wanting to please them, doesn't he? Bob was right when he said this line is a departure from last year's. And we've done that before. We'll do it again. Lucky Lad's marketing strategy is to be first. You remember that we started the surfer look with the bright stripes, and by the time our competitors caught up we had introduced the safari look in olives and tans. Everybody else is doing safari this year. We're setting the new style, which we call neon lights. And, as you might imagine, our designers are looking at what will replace this one when our competitors are producing it.

"Let me tell you about Claude and why he's here. Several months ago I found myself with an hour to kill between appointments. I called the office and there were no urgent matters, so I decided to walk around and get some fresh air.

"Knowing we would be opening our retail stores, I went into several stores, and in every store the scenario was about the same. I received the standard, 'May I help you?' and then I was left alone to fend for myself. In one store I saw a T-shirt that I thought would be perfect as a gift I needed, but I couldn't find a salesperson after I found the shirt, so I left.

"Later, I walked into a shop looking for the same shirt, and that's when I met Claude. To make a long story short, instead of buying a ten-dollar T-shirt, I left there with four, thirty dollar sweatshirts. Walking to my next appointment, I began asking myself what had happened. Why had I gone into this store wanting a ten-dollar shirt and left having spent ten times as much? What had the salesperson said or done? Who had trained him to be so effective, and what techniques had he used? All I could recall was talking to the salesperson and then agreeing to buy the four shirts.

"About a week later it was still bothering me, so I went back to the store and the owner was the only person there. He greeted me with, 'May I help you?' and then left me alone. At that point I knew it was the salesperson, not the store, that held the secret.

"You all know Martha and Jennifer who work for me. I sent them down there, described the salesperson and asked them to try not to buy. When they walked back into the office with sacks, now that's 'sacks,' plural, I knew we needed this person."

Claude was hearing this story for the first time. In their conversations George had mentioned checking Claude out, but Claude had not known the whole story until now.

George continued, "We are going into a highly competitive market where more people fail or break-even than succeed. We are going after the volatile retail clothing dollar. Since we cannot expect to succeed using a 'me too' approach, we're going to try it Claude's way. After spending hours with him I have reduced his method of selling to a fairly simple formula. In fact I have reduced it to one piece of paper, and I'm going to ask Claude to pass these out."

George handed Claude a stack of laminated sheets of paper, and Claude began passing them out. After everyone had a chance to look it over, George spoke again.

"The principle is very simple and is written across the top of the page: 'Never Take Money From A Stranger.' We have discussed relationship selling before, and now we're going to a deeper level to determine what that relationship will be even before we meet the customer. All of our activities with a customer will be based on satisfying that customer's needs and desires, in the same way we would for any good friend or relative.

"Also listed on this sheet are the rules by which we will play. Let's go over them. Rule number one is, 'Always greet the customer with a question, but never let it be the 'May I help you?' question. I'm going to insist on this one. If anyone walks into one of our stores and is greeted with the question, 'May I help you?' by one of our salespeople, that salesperson stands to lose his or her job. I'm that serious.

"Rule number two is, 'Whatever you want to say to a customer, phrase it in the form of a question.' I've watched Claude use this over and over, and it works. The human mind responds to questions automatically—we can't seem to stop that process. And as long as we're the ones asking the questions, we're in control of the inter-action.

"Rule number three is, 'Anyone who will buy once will buy more than once, so sell them now.' By the time you get to know someone well enough to take their money, you should know them well enough to help them solve several problems or to satisfy more than one desire.

"Claude's job is to help each of us sell. He's going to ride with each of us, work in all of our stores showing our salespeople how to sell. He'll go with us as we call on buyers.

"Now, I'm not suggesting that Claude has all the an-swers. All we're doing here is trying a unique approach to our market: displaying an honest and sincere desire to help."

After the meeting several of the better salespeople made appointments to have Claude come and help them. They were the winners, the ones who were always looking for a way to improve their success. The others were still skeptical.

That night in his apartment, Claude took out the red notebook, read several passages, and then added a line to his page.

Losers Decide What *They* Want And Then Take It, Winners Learn What Others Want and Help Them Have It.